THE CAREGIVER'S MISSION

A COMPREHENSIVE PRACTICAL GUIDE ON CARING FOR YOUR ELDERLY PARENT, SPOUSE, OR FAMILY MEMBER

by

Steven Ross

dp
DISTINCTIVE PUBLISHING CORP.

The Caregiver's Mission
By Steven Ross
Copyright 1993 by Steven Ross

Published by Distinctive Publishing Corp.
PO Box 17868
Plantation, Florida 33318-7868
Printed in the United States of America

ISBN: 0-942963-41-5
Library of Congress No.: 93-24305
Price: $12.95

Library of Congress Cataloging-in-Publication Data

Ross, Steven, 1960-
     The caregiver's mission : a comprehensive practical guide on
caring for your elderly parent, spouse, or family member / by
Steven Ross.
          p.   cm.
     ISBN 0-942963-41-5 (tradesoft) : $12.95
     1. Aged—Care—United States. 2. Aged—Health and hygiene—
United States. 3. Aged—Services for—United States. 4. Adult
children—United States. 5. Caregivers—United States. I. Title.
HV1461.R67   1993
362.6—dc20   93-24305
                                                  CIP

To my mom and dad,
"Ema & Aba,"
for all you have given
to see your children succeed.
We hope only that some day,
in your old age,
we are able to return this love to you.

THE CAREGIVER'S CREED

At the close of the day
When I'm at my wit's end,
I will pray and have faith
To start over again.
Each day I'll face care
As a challenge that's new
And remember I've done
The best I can do.

When I ask myself why
Or how long this will last,
I'll remember the love
That's been shared in the past.
I know I'll have days
That are lonely and sad.
It is then I'll remember
Good times that we had.
I won't be a martyr
Or do it alone.
When I need someone's help
I will pick up the phone.

Opinions I'll get
And sometimes a fight,
But I will not feel guilty
If I think I am right.
I know how things are,
For I'm there every day,
So I won't be upset
When they question what I say.

I won't lose myself
In my every day tasks
Or hide how I feel
With the caregiver's mask –
A mask that protects
Fear and anger inside me,
That if vented and worked through
Would be tools that could guide me.

It may seem what I do
Is never enough,
So I won't set a standard
That's so very tough.
A little each day
May be all to be gained;
I'll accept any progress
And not feel it's in vain.

A step taken forward,
A word that is spoken,
To recall from a memory
That for years has been broken,
Are all little victories
In a caregiver's day
That we should rejoice in
Each night. Every day.

STEVEN ROSS

Throughout the book I may have taken the liberty of using she or her to refer to an elderly person. This use of gender was meant only for ease of reading, even though the majority of the elderly are female. Perhaps it is just a phenomenon of nature that the females are the hardier of our species! I have also taken the liberty of focusing on adult children of elderly parents as the caregivers in this book. This book is just as valuable to spouses, friends and loved ones who are caregivers for the elderly. I chose to focus on women as caregivers because it is usually the daughter or daughter-in-law of the family who assumes the caregiving role.

TABLE OF CONTENTS

INTRODUCTION

THERE IS AN INTERESTING FAMILY PATTERN emerging in America today. As a professional in the field of aging, I see it acted out daily.

Hard working, caring women and men who were in the past only expected to be parents to their children, are now expected to also assume a parenting role with their parents. With people living into the eighth and ninth decades of life, wedding vows taken years in the past to care for a spouse in sickness and in health are, by necessity, being kept.

As children we were naturally taught the skills, values and roles needed to become responsible members of society. We were taught to be good students, good citizens, good workers and good moms and dads, but where in our upbringing were we educated on how to care for an aging, dependent parent or spouse? Who are our role models and how do we know what is expected of us?

For some, the caregiver's mission may seem easy. For most, I suspect that this mission is a daily struggle for emotional, physical and financial survival. The perceived need for support, help, and accurate information is what inspired the writing of this book. My hope is to make everyone's challenge a little easier while strengthening the bonds of love and understanding between the generations.

1

THE MISSION

*May we be blessed with the gifts of patience, love and compassion
for the elderly, and may the spirit of healing be within us,
so that we may comfort those entrusted to our care.*

The morning began with cries from the bedroom. As I entered the room I found her in a wet diaper, needing comfort and care. It was difficult for me to calm my loved one because of her inability to communicate. A loving touch and a gentle caress of the hair seemed to calm her a little. After a diaper change it was time for the morning meal. I spoon fed her with great difficulty. At times she would push my hand away and spit the food on the floor. After about forty-five minutes, I believed that she'd had enough to sustain her for the morning, so I decided it was time to get her dressed and up for the day. Picking out her clothing was easy. Putting her clothes on her was another story. After a bit of a struggle, the job was done. I wiped the sweat from my brow and took her into the family room. As I worked in the den, I watched to be sure she would be O.K. There is always the possibility of her getting hurt, so I'm afraid to leave her alone for even a minute.

No wonder I'm exhausted at the end of the day. My life seems to revolve around this person for whom I'm caring. As I worked in the den, however, I thought to myself how someday it would all be worthwhile. My one-year-old daughter will grow up to be a beautiful young lady, a productive member of society who may even take care of me in my old age.

Surprised? Well, don't be. Those caring for an aging, dependent parent or spouse may have been led to believe that I was describing a typical morning of a caregiver. Others would have correctly thought that this was a typical morning of a mother caring for her young child.

What is the difference between caring for an aging, dependent parent and a very young child, if the tasks appear to be the same? The difference is in our perception of the ultimate outcome of caregiving and our expectations of what can and should be done. A young, dependent child will grow stronger and more independent, while an elderly loved one may become

1

progressively more dependent and debilitated. In both cases there is the same need for love, patience and understanding. In caring for the child, one needs to be knowledgeable about the developmental process. The new parent has access to an overwhelming amount of information and resources in the form of books, tapes, and professional guidance. Even if this information is unavailable, a new parent can always call a friend, family member or professional and ask advice on what to do if the baby has gas, can't sleep or is running a fever.

Those caring for an elderly loved one may not be so fortunate. Things may seem to get worse, and there may be nobody to turn to for help and guidance. Even people who try to help may not always be able to meet the needs of the elderly loved one and caregiver. How do some caregivers cope well, while others have so much trouble? So many times I have heard the pain of children or spouses who feel that they haven't done enough for their elderly loved one. No matter how hard I try, I am unable to soothe their guilt and anger. They believe that "the golden years" are a time for peace and enjoyment of life, and they can't understand or accept the hardships that may accompany aging.

Caregivers who cope well understand the challenge before them. They have faith in difficult times; they know when to give up and when to push ahead. They take a negative situation and see the positive side of things. They have a plan of what to do and what to expect, should a need arise. They learn how to negotiate complicated governmental, social service and medical systems to obtain the help they need. They accept help when offered and learn to know whom they can trust and depend upon. They have a good understanding of nature, the aging process and the human body. They are eager to learn from the experience of others and are comfortable sharing their feelings of frustration, fear and anger.

A successful caregiver accepts credit for a job well done and is proud of even a minor caregiving accomplishment. Most of all, successful caregivers survive daily setbacks and problems of a caregiving relationship by knowing in their hearts that they have entered into a sacred relationship filled with ups and downs, joys and pain, life and death—a relationship that will never be forgotten or regretted if the caregiver can see her importance and worth. Our mission is a difficult one, but we must go forth with love, strength and pride, knowing that perhaps someday we will understand and be thankful that we've had the opportunity to care for an elderly loved one in need.

2

A PERSPECTIVE ON AGING

Many adult children of aging parents have shared with me their concerns and worries about mothers and fathers. What is very difficult for the caregiver and the aging parent to accept and deal with is the decline in physical ability and function. When I have done intake interviews for nursing home placements, adult children are often alarmed about how their parents may be deteriorating. This is especially true for children who live far away and only see their parents at three- or four-month intervals. An adult child may make a visit in the summer and find Mom or Dad having a little trouble getting around, then visit again at Christmas and find that Mom or Dad has lost weight, is barely walking, and is not taking care of things in the home. The difference you may see in your elderly parent between her seventy-fifth and seventy-sixth birthday may seem very minor, compared to the differences you observe between her eighty-ninth and ninetieth birthdays. Only one year has passed in both cases. The one-year difference at the very end of the life cycle can be dramatic, and it is sometimes shocking for adult children to witness. If you put it all in a life span perspective, it doesn't seem so surprising. Look at the difference between a one-year-old and a two-year-old when it comes to the ability to move around and communicate. From crawling to walking to one word and talking, all in the span of one year.

Have you ever asked a child how old she is? Usually a nine-year-old will tell you that she is nine and a half or almost ten. It is nearly universal that children want the status of being older, growing bigger and gaining more privileges. When you ask young or middle aged adults their age, you will usually get a response that is rounded down a few years. When you ask very old people their age, they seem to be proud and actually round up. Many of my friends in their nineties are proud to have lived so long, and they tell me that they are almost one hundred years old when I ask.

3

Life seems to be a cycle. I have taught children martial arts and seen their energy, speed, vigor and resilience. I have spent the majority of my adult professional career working with the very, very old. In later stages one loses the energy, speed, vigor and resilience of youth.

At birth one grows and develops. Growth and development occur differently among children. Your child may learn to walk faster than your neighbor's child. Your neighbor's child may be shorter than your child until age thirteen and then rapidly grow and surpass everyone in the neighborhood. Just as children develop at different rates, there is some variability in how people in their later years decline in function. The elderly are quite a heterogeneous group of people. Not only do different people age at different rates, different organs in the body such as the heart and lungs may also age and decline at different rates. You see examples of the variability of the elderly every day. Many eighty-year-old people are out golfing and swimming every day, while their counterparts may be confined to a bed in a nursing home, unable to walk. What accounts for or explains the variability in how people age? I wish I had the answer. Chances are, however, there is more than one answer to this question.

No one theory adequately explains the changes and declines in function that we experience with aging. The effects of aging may be viewed as a combination of biological and chemical events that occur over the life span. In other words, no one factor alone can explain the variability in how people age. Some believe that aging is due to an accumulation of environmental insults that one experiences during life. Others view the aging process as being controlled by genetic factors. Those adhering to the latter hypothesis believe that our length of life and decline in function is genetically predetermined. Humans in general have a specific life span, as do monkeys, dogs, horses and grasshoppers. Perhaps our genes determine how long we are going to live. Whatever causes us to age is not entirely in our control. Maybe it is a blessing that we can't control how long we live as a species. The human race may not yet be prepared to have such knowledge. Even if we can't control our genetically predetermined life span, it is possible to live a lifestyle that may prevent or delay certain diseases. Healthful diet, exercise, restful sleep and avoidance of cigarettes and excessive alcohol consumption all can contribute to a better quality of life.

As a caregiver of an aging parent, you don't necessarily have to become an expert on the diseases and disabilities that your loved one may experience. What you need to do is to be able to recognize what is normal and expected and what is abnormal and part of a disease process. You also need to gain an understanding of your loved one's needs and ability to perform such basic activities as getting to the bathroom, moving around the environment, managing personal hygiene, taking medications, using the phone, cooking, eating and managing areas of daily life.

Take a moment to visualize how it feels to be older and physically challenged. Perhaps getting up from the couch to get a drink of water can take several minutes. Walking from the bedroom to the bathroom may seem like an eternity. Once in the bathroom, just getting on and off the toilet may be a painful, difficult task. We all take such simple daily activities for granted until our ability to negotiate our environment is hampered by age-associated disability or illness.

Many of the losses that occur with aging are not as sudden as we imagine. Difficulty walking in an eighty-year-old may have developed slowly, with the onset of arthritis, over several years. Many elderly people adapt to their disabilities and simply restrict activities or adhere to a set routine and daily ritual of planned activities. As caregivers we need to be sensitive to the changes our loved ones experience, and we shouldn't be too quick to give up or not pursue answers to concerns just because of our loved one's advanced age. A perfect example of this concept is a conversation I observed between a young doctor and his elderly patient at the nursing home. During the visit, the patient, a ninety-year-old gentleman, told the doctor that his left shoulder hurt quite a bit. The physician responded to the complaint of pain by telling the ninety-year-old patient that he should expect pain in his shoulder at ninety years of age. The patient responded very wisely to the physician by saying that his right shoulder was also ninety years old, and it didn't hurt. "Obviously," said the patient, "something must be wrong with my left shoulder." While the example may seem silly, the concept is not far from the truth. The majority of illnesses seen in older age groups is chronic in nature; if they are properly assessed and treated, they may respond well. The caregiver should not give up just because there is no cure. Our goal as caregivers is to assist our elderly loved ones to function at the highest level possible, while avoiding premature and unnecessary disability.

3

THE EFFECT OF ELDER CARE
ON THE CAREGIVER
AND FAMILY

CARING FOR AN ELDERLY PARENT IS A TASK that affects the individual caregiver and the caregiver's family. Friends and onlookers may not fully understand and comprehend the emotional stress and energy that goes into caring for a frail, elderly parent. Many times it is not the physical tasks or time taken from the caregiver's life that has the greatest impact. It is the emotions and feelings of fear, anger, resentment, hopelessness, frustration, sadness, bewilderment and unfairness that make the caregiving relationship so difficult. Recognizing and effectively working through and dealing with your feelings as a caregiver will tremendously help you get through the process. The goal of this chapter is to help you recognize how you are feeling and learn how you can deal with these feelings. Sometimes recognizing your feelings is the most difficult part of the caregiving relationship. Many caregivers suppress how they truly feel in order to protect themselves and their elderly parent from discomfort. Others inappropriately take out their frustrations about caring for an elderly parent on other family members, friends and co-workers, not recognizing why they do it. Some caregivers stoically suffer alone until they reach the point of burnout.

We all cope differently with the stresses and challenges that life deals us. Many challenges and stresses pass quickly, and we adjust. Caring for an elderly parent or parents may, however, be a process that lasts for years. You may spend three years caring for an elderly father who suffered a stroke, and after his death, face another five years caring for your mother, who has Alzheimer's disease. Eight years of caregiving is not a passing stress that one can ignore; one must actively work on adjusting to it. Yet, how many of us actually prepare, address and work on our feelings about caring for elderly parents? I can tell you from my experience that many children caring for elderly parents could drastically improve the quality of their lives and that of their parents just by recognizing and getting help with the "Feeling Aspect" of the caregiving relationship. If you are a caregiver, I am sure that you have interacted with many health care professionals who have offered information on diseases, medications, visiting nurses, home health aides, home delivered meals and other physical support services available to assist in the care of your elderly parent. How many of these health care professionals have given you a big hug and asked how you were feeling and coping with the caregiving relationship? If any of them have, consider yourself blessed, because many professionals just don't have the time or the expertise to assist caregivers in this way. Much of the support you receive will be through informal support systems that you develop with family and friends and through your own soul searching.

Let's do some soul searching now. Listed below are some common feelings and thoughts shared by many caregivers. Take a few moments and respond to the issues that relate to you or your situation. If the challenges below are affecting you or your family, take the time to explore and understand how to better cope. Depending on whether you are the spouse or adult child of an elderly loved one, some statements may not apply to you. You may want to answer these questions today and answer again at a later point in time, after you have fully digested the information in this book and are coping more effectively. You might find it interesting to measure how your feelings and outlook have changed for the better, by comparing the two sets of responses. Often the help of a professional is valuable in resolving the concerns that are so common to caregivers.

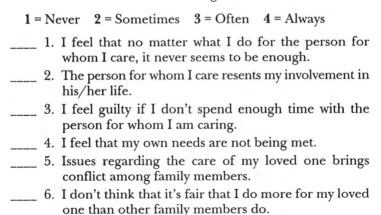

1 = Never   2 = Sometimes   3 = Often   4 = Always

_____ 1. I feel that no matter what I do for the person for whom I care, it never seems to be enough.

_____ 2. The person for whom I care resents my involvement in his/her life.

_____ 3. I feel guilty if I don't spend enough time with the person for whom I am caring.

_____ 4. I feel that my own needs are not being met.

_____ 5. Issues regarding the care of my loved one brings conflict among family members.

_____ 6. I don't think that it's fair that I do more for my loved one than other family members do.

_____ 7. Caring for my loved one interferes with my personal life.

_____ 8. Caring for my elderly parent interferes with my own marriage and family life.

_____ 9. Family relationships have become more difficult since the illness or dependence of my loved one.

_____10. I don't seem to have time to take care of myself anymore.

_____11. I feel that my choices are limited and that I am stuck in this situation.

_____12. I feel that my caregiving situation is stressful.

_____13. I am scared and feel helpless about my caregiving situation.

_____14. I feel guilty asking for help from others when it comes to caring for my elderly family member.

_____15. I don't feel that I am doing much good for my elderly loved one.

_____16. I question my judgment and wonder if I am providing the proper care for my elderly loved one.

_____17. I am not sure where to go for help.

_____18. Since becoming a caregiver, I am anxious.

_____19. Since becoming a caregiver, I feel sad.

_____20. Since becoming a caregiver, I easily get angry.

_____21. Since becoming a caregiver, I am tired and have no energy.

_____22. Since becoming a caregiver, I have lost contact with friends.

_____23. Since becoming a caregiver, I don't do the things that I used to enjoy.

_____24. I get angry or lose patience with the person for whom I am caring.

_____25. I get frustrated and just feel like giving up.

_____26. When I get angry, I hold the anger inside and get physically ill.

_____27. It hurts me to see my elderly loved one grow increasingly frail.

_____28. I feel like my elderly loved one uses his/her illness or disability to manipulate me or other family members.

_____29. When the person for whom I am caring is not well, I feel the need to fix the problem.

____30. I feel powerless to help my elderly loved one.

____31. I feel responsible for the happiness of the person for whom I am caring.

____32. When I need help, I feel as though there is no place to turn.

____33. I worry about the future.

____34. My personal well-being suffers as a result of being a caregiver.

____35. I feel that I owe a debt to the person for whom I am caring because she/he once took such good care of me.

____36. My friends and/or family just don't understand what I am going through.

____37. The person for whom I am caring was never really good to me and I resent having to care for him/her now.

____38. I am uncomfortable assuming the caregiving or dominant role with the person for whom I am caring.

____39. I don't understand what is happening with the person for whom I am caring.

____40. I have unanswered questions about the medical conditions and prognosis of my elderly loved one.

____41. I feel uncertain about the future and I don't know what to expect.

____42. I feel that I am not prepared to face what the future might bring.

____43. Communicating with the person for whom I am caring is difficult.

____44. I feel guilty when I have to say no to the person for whom I am caring.

____45. I feel guilty because I don't want my elderly loved one to live with me.

____46. I have never been close with the person for whom I am caring and I feel like I need to get closer before he/she dies.

____47. I would feel guilty if I had to put my elderly loved one in a nursing home.

____48. I worry about my elderly loved one dying.

____49. I think it would be a relief if the person for whom I am caring would die, and feeling this way makes me uncomfortable.

____50. I worry about how we will pay for care and services.

____51. I feel like I have someone I can confide in and trust.

____52. I derive satisfaction from caring for my loved one.

____53. Since I have been a caregiver, I feel that I have become close to the one for whom I am caring.

____54. I feel good about being a caregiver.

____55. Caregiving gives me a sense of satisfaction.

____56. I feel proud when we experience caregiving accomplishments.

____57. Being a caregiver has brought out stengths in me that I never knew I had.

____58. I am a natural caregiver and I have always been that way.

____59. I feel that being a caregiver has made me a better person.

____60. If I could change or improve five things about my caregiving situation, these five things would be—and I would change them by doing the following:

1._____

2._____

3._____

4._____

5._____

Let's take some time to explore the many feelings that accompany the relationships with our dependent elderly parents. When I developed this feeling inventory, I simply wrote down statements that caregivers have shared with me over the years. The interesting thing is that almost all caregivers may have these feelings at some point in their caregiving relationship. Negative feelings can be changed by simply looking at each situation in a different way. Changing your perceptions and outlook can be the most difficult task you will experience as a caregiver. Perhaps the only task that will be more difficult will be changing the perceptions of your elderly dependent parent. This brings us to the exploration of the first statement in the caregiver's inventory: **No matter what I do for the person for whom I am caring, it is never enough.** If you believe this statement applies to you, there may be several reasons why you are feeling this way. The first reason deals with the reality of growing older and frail. Sometimes there is NOTHING ANYONE CAN DO TO MAKE YOUR ELDERLY LOVED ONE BETTER. The best doctors, food, vitamins, medicine, exercise and scientific inventions cannot reverse the natural aging process. Actually, sometimes doing too much to, or for, elderly people worsens their conditions. It isn't easy to give up and accept that nothing can be done to cure or reverse the frailties of old age, and I'm not suggesting that we can't offer comfort, love and every chance for recovery to our elderly loved ones. Just don't blame yourself for not doing enough when everything you can humanly do may realistically never make Mom or Dad well again. Not every aspect of your parent's care is in your control. Once you recognize this and relinquish responsibility that is not realistic, you will cope much more effectively. In order for us to measure how we are doing, we often need some standard of comparison. As caregivers we have difficulty measuring how well we are doing because we have no real standard against which to measure our performance. We certainly can't measure how we are doing by our parent's physical and emotional functioning. Caregivers who feel that *whatever they do is never enough* often base this feeling on the declines that Mom or Dad are experiencing. Elderly people decline. This is nature. Don't measure your success as a caregiver by your parent's life condition. Doing the best you can do is enough, and you need to accept this. You will not be perfect, nor will you be able to be super human every day. Look at your standards and caregiving expectations closely; if they are not in harmony with reality, think about adjusting them.

Now ask yourself this question: Are my feelings that *whatever I do is never enough* just internally based, or are they based on input which I am getting from friends, family and elderly parents? To some elderly parents who are lonely and isolated, a son or daughter is the sole reason for living. If your elderly parent's focus and life are based upon contact and interaction with you, there is a good chance that in your parent's eyes *no matter what you do, it will never be enough*.

Think about it. What a tremendous responsibility it is to be the sole reason for another person's surviving, especially when that person is a parent. If your elderly parent views you as the sole reason for living, things may be O.K. when your parent is happy and content with your relationship. When you don't come through for your parent as expected, the emphasis that your elderly parent may place upon even minor events may be exaggerated. Just being aware of the value your elderly parent places upon your relationship may be helpful when you feel that whatever you do, it is never enough. Maybe you can be everything to everybody for a little while, but in a short period of time you may reach a point where there is nothing left to give. If you allow yourself to reach this point, neither you nor your elderly parent will benefit.

Learn to communicate your needs to your elderly parent, and share your feelings in a positive way. Set boundaries and limits, and agree on what should be expected in the caregiving relationship. Look for the feelings behind what your elderly parent is saying.

If you visit your mother twice a week and she says that you don't visit enough, instead of arguing with her, respond by saying something like, "Mom, twice a week is the most I can visit right now. You are very important to me and I want to spend as much time with you as possible. It seems to me that maybe you are lonely, and that is why you want me to come over every day. Because it is impossible for me to visit every day, what other ways can we explore to help you with your feelings of loneliness?"

The feeling behind the behavior of wanting daily visits is loneliness. It is important for you as a caregiver to recognize this and work with your parent on ways of handling the loneliness, rather than **feeling guilty about not spending enough time with your parent or not doing enough**.

It is extremely difficult to try to help an elderly parent if she/he is **resentful** of your efforts. Resentment may assume many ugly faces. Your parent may be angry and resist your attempts to help. He/she may be critical of your efforts and tell you to mind your own business. Your parent may even turn anger inward and become depressed and isolated. Why do we resent people who are trying to help us? If we don't want any help or believe that help is not needed, resentment may develop toward those who wish to come to our aide. If we have delicate egos, perhaps accepting help makes us feel inadequate in some way. You may resent accepting help if you feel that you can give nothing back in return, and you may resent help if the person helping you doesn't do so in a gracious manner. When you are older and growing dependent upon family and friends for assistance, the smallest issue may become disproportionately significant. At your age and with your busy family and work schedule, you would probably welcome having a housekeeper come to your house and clean or cook for you. It would be a privilege that many working adults can't afford. If you were to offer to have such help brought to your elderly mother's house, she might show resentment. The resentment would not be because she is ungrateful. Her reaction might be based on her fear of growing dependent and frail; she might fear the need for assistance for things that she has always done well and enjoyed all her life. If your mom was a homemaker for fifty years, always doing things around the house her way, imagine the significance your attempt to bring in a housekeeper would have on her self-esteem. She may very well be resentful; as a caregiver you need to recognize this. If you don't recognize the feelings beneath your elderly parent's actions, the resentment may lead to anger and withdrawal on your part.

If you feel uncomfortable asking your parent to do something that is in her best interest when she doesn't want to do it, resentment may be the outcome. A major issue in caring for an elderly parent is figuring out what *the best interest* is. When we were teenagers, our parents may have believed that it was in our best interest that we *not* go out with a certain boyfriend or girlfriend. We resented them for this, and the more they insisted that this girlfriend/boyfriend wasn't good for us, the more we wanted to go out with her/him. Maybe our parent's evaluation was correct and maybe it was not. The battle was over control of our destiny and gaining autonomy and independence as a teenager maturing into adulthood. Now the tides are turned, and we find ourselves in a similar struggle with our elderly parents. Only this time the struggle is for our parents' autonomy and independence—a struggle that we shouldn't take lightly. Sometimes the more we push our wills upon our parents, the more they will resist—or even worse, the more they will concede and become unnecessarily dependent upon us for daily decisions. If at all possible, try to provide options rather than giving directions. You may be more comfortable with directing your elderly parent's care if you provide options while you are doing what is in her best interest.

The illness or dependency of an elderly parent or spouse has an effect on the entire family. How an individual caregiver or family unit copes depends upon many variables. Family dynamics are always changing as family members cope with individual issues and family relationships. I have worked with many families who communicate well and are supportive, loving and cohesive.

I have worked with other families that communicate poorly or not at all and are destructive to themselves and their elderly parents. Every family has history, both secret and open, which people outside the family may share. My staff and I know that when we admit an elderly person to our nursing center, we are also admitting the family. Many times the elderly person receiving care copes better than the family caregiver who is offering the assistance. If **caregiving of an elderly parent brings conflict among family members,** interferes with personal, marriage and family life, and doesn't allow you time or energy to care for yourself, you need to take the time to carefully address and work through these issues.

Conflict among siblings of elderly parents can be disabling for the family, especially when important decisions must be made. In all families, each individual member has a unique way of fitting in and coping. Cultural values and the style elderly parents used to raise the children all contribute to the development of the caregiving relationship as the generations age. The oldest may be the one looked upon to assume the care of an elderly parent. The youngest child or the daughters may provide most of the actual hands-on care. Daughters-in-law may substitute for the sons who can't cope with caring for elderly parents. Estranged family may want nothing to do with an elderly parent until it is time to distribute the assets and settle the will after death. You may be an only child facing the care of an elderly parent alone, or you may be one of several children who are able to assist. Elderly parents may pit one child against the other and cause conflict, or children may compete to gain the recognition of an elderly parent. The scenarios are as varied as families' composition and history.

Relationships with spouses, parents and siblings are constantly changing. Your goal should be to develop these relationships each day through communication, trust and mutual support. If you see that relationships are deteriorating, don't wait for them to get better on their own. Families caring for elderly parents especially need to evaluate and work on relationships. I recommend counseling for many families that are dealing with the stress of elderly parent care. Many issues in families are deeper than what appears on the surface, and there may be a need to work through these matters before the family can care for an elderly parent in a unified way. Referrals to a marriage and family therapist, psychologist or social worker may be made through your physician or local mental health agency. Family support groups may also be available to assist families in coping with the care of an elderly parent. Check with local hospitals, senior centers, nursing homes and social service agencies to see if such groups are in place in your area.

Unity in a family caring for an elderly dependent parent is very important. If one child is wanting to put a parent in a nursing home while another is doing everything possible to keep the parent at home, there will be obvious disharmony. The children will spend more time attempting to work through their own conflict rather than attempting to assist the needy parent. Resolution of conflict is not always easy in families caring for aging parents. I have found that there are usually one or two children that are very involved in the day to day caregiving; these involved children have realistic expectations. There may, however, be another child who is a bit removed from the family; he/she may work against the efforts of the hands-on siblings. Elderly parents may go along with the unrealistic child's thoughts because they are hearing what they want to hear, not necessarily what is good for them.

One sibling may act with her heart while the other acts with her head. Conflict often arises between the thinkers and the feelers if good communication doesn't exist. The family caring for an elderly parent must spend regular time doing the following:

- Meet in a comfortable setting at least once a month and have open discussion. Include your elderly parent if possible.
- Be sure that every family member has a clear idea of what the parent's needs are.
- Be sure that there are clear goals and expectations for the care of a parent.
- Be sure that tasks and responsibilities are distributed among family members. Responsibilities should be divided according to what each family member is comfortable with and able to do. Regularly review and redistribute responsibilities if a family member becomes overburdened.
- Discuss any problems or misunderstandings that have developed over the past weeks, and attempt to resolve them and prevent them from recurring.
- Discuss how your parent and the family has done since the last meeting, and evaluate the success of meeting caregiving goals.
- Take time to share positive family developments unrelated to the care of your aging parent that have occurred since the last meeting.

I know that the steps I have outlined above may be difficult for even the most functional cohesive family to follow. I also understand that geographical distance, disputes and personal agendas may stand in the way of such family meetings. Do what you can to build a bridge between your brothers and sisters. Give them a copy of this book if they are willing to read it. Believe me when I say that several hours of working on family relationships in the beginning of the caregiving mission is well worth the time and will save countless hours and days of worrying about family problems had the issues never been resolved.

It would take several chapters to go through each statement in the caregiver's inventory, so I want to focus on the single most important issue. **THE ISSUE IS YOU AND YOUR SURVIVAL.** I don't mean surviving in a physical way. I mean survival in a spiritual sense. Physically, caregivers often find it within themselves to do the tasks. The shopping, driving, and physical assistance that is required to care for an elderly parent is done by the caregiver or by hired help if the caregiver is fortunate enough to have the resources. Personal lives, family relationships and marriages can dissolve under the stress of caring for an elderly parent when people are without spiritual support and foundation.

When caring for a dependent parent, one soon realizes that many things are not in our human control. We try our best to control the situation, but at times it may become overwhelming. Among caregivers with whom I have worked, those who have faith in God or a higher being are the ones who seem to cope more effectively. These caregivers simply do what is humanly possible and turn the outcome over to God. They tell me that God cannot work through them if they don't let Him or if they shut Him out for putting them in their particular position. I have seen a lot of human suffering, caring for the elderly, especially the elderly who are stuck in a place between life and death.

How do some caregivers deal with being stuck and having the feeling that there is no way out of their situation? They deal with feeling stuck by turning matters over to God. I had a very dear lady who lived at the retirement community I directed. She would see me weekly, and we would visit. Her husband was severely impaired with Alzheimer's disease and didn't even recognize her. They had been married almost fifty years, and she had a terrible time adjusting to being physically and emotionally separated from her husband. To compound things, this lady's health and eyesight were failing. Every time we would visit she would cry and wonder why her life was as it was. She cared for her husband for quite a while by herself, until it became impossible for her, physically. She did such a good job caring for him that many of the other residents didn't recognize how impaired her husband was. When she could no longer care for him and he was transferred to the health center, she felt relieved, but she was left without a purpose. They were still married, but unfortunately he didn't recognize her, and she couldn't bear to visit him. Every time she would visit me she would cry, and before getting up to leave she would say that the good Lord was blessing her to let her live in such a place and have such good friends. When her husband died, I knew what was coming. She took to bed and ended up in the hospital. It appeared as though she had just given up and wanted to die. The difficulty was that she was stuck, and she wasn't sure what she wanted. She felt that there was nothing to live for, yet her body wasn't ready to die. Like many others in her position, she curtailed her eating and lost a lot of weight. About three weeks after her husband died, I visited her in the nursing home and asked how she was. She held my hand and said that she didn't know what to do. She was stuck in an awful position. She didn't have the will to live, yet she wasn't sick enough to die. We sat and prayed together that morning for just a few moments, and before I left she turned matters over to God. I saw her a few days later and she seemed very peaceful. Smiling, she asked me for a drink of water. Before I left, she said, "Thank you, honey," as she always did. The next day she died. I have no doubt that she was helped to exit this world by turning matters over to God.

When you feel stressed out, overburdened, out of control, angry or just like giving up, close your eyes and ask God for help and spiritual guidance. He will help if you just let Him. The power of prayer and one's relationship with God is very important when you are undergoing the stress of a caregiving relationship. I am always amazed at how deeply ingrained prayer can be in our lives. A prime example is a lady we took care of in our nursing home who had severe memory loss and anxiety. She always looked so scared and anxious. If you left her alone she would cry for help and just repeat, "Help me! I'm so scared and miserable." Nothing anyone could do would soothe her, and I honestly believe that the minute you left she forgot that you were just there visiting her. One day she was crying and nobody could console her. When I walked in the room, I held her hand and whispered in her ear, in a very soft voice, "Our Father Who Art in Heaven..." Much to my surprise, she remembered and finished the whole prayer for me. From that day forward when she was crying, I would whisper those six words to her—"Our Father Who Art in Heaven"—and she would finish the prayer and calm down.

If we think and pray with our heart, we can always find positives in the most distressful and sad situation. Through prayer God can grant you peace, patience and compassion. Through prayer your caregiving relationship can be satisfying to you and your loved one.

I believe it's important to include some guidance in this book on the subject of GUILT. Guilt is a feeling that so many caregivers have shared with me. Guilt is a feeling that people should express when a moral offense is committed. If one does something to purposefully harm another, then guilt is an appropriate feeling. Perhaps guilt keeps humans from doing anything they want whenever they want. The feeling of guilt may be related to one's individual conscience or personal sense of what is right or wrong. I have seen adult children purposely harm and take advantage of elderly parents and feel no remorse or guilt. I have also seen caregivers who go above and beyond human expectations and still feel guilty. The opposite of guilt is innocence. Innocence implies that you have done nothing wrong, at least intentionally. Whatever burden you are carrying, follow this formula and you may feel better.

FAITH + PRAYER - (GUILT) + FORGIVENESS = <u>RELIEF</u>

It is a formula that I prescribe to all caregivers in need of relief. You cannot be responsible for the happiness of your elderly parent, nor can you be responsible for bad things that happen if you are doing your best and your intentions are good. Tough decisions about living arrangements, finance, independence, medical care, and even life and death may need to be made. Guilt can paralyze your decision making ability and cause unnecessary worry. The energy you spend worrying or feeling guilty is taking away from positive energy that you could be spending with yourself, your family and your elderly loved one. There will be times when you feel like giving up. There will be times when you get angry and stressed. There will be times when you feel powerless and at the end of your rope. There will be times when you feel that you should do more or that you don't want to do any more at all. There will be times when families will fight, and times when you will say or do something that you later regret. FAITH IS WHAT KEEPS US GOING IN ROUGH TIMES. You gain faith through prayer. You gain peace and lose guilt through forgiveness. When you can master the formula I have outlined, you can share it with your elderly parent; together, you can work on resolving hurts that were buried between you over the many years that you have shared. Think about it; nobody on this earth, while your parents are alive, will ever have known you longer. If you have issues that need to be discussed and worked through, take the time to do it now, at the bedside, rather than after death at the graveside. Family histories don't end upon the death of the oldest of the generation. When your parent dies, you may be left with unresolved problems, fears, and hurts that will be carried on for generations to come. Work through issues now, and perhaps some day you will protect your child from the grief that you now may be experiencing.

Before ending this chapter I feel obligated to recommend that caregivers and elderly people who are receiving care get counseling through rough times. A good marriage and family therapist, gerontologist, social worker, psychologist or pastoral counselor can do a great deal to help families through caregiving issues. Support groups for caregivers are also valuable. It is difficult to ask for help or admit that you can't do it on your own. Don't let pride or embarrassment hinder your ability to survive and succeed.

4

PREVENTION OF FALLS AND HIP FRACTURES— HOME SAFETY

When Mom called the first time, I wasn't so concerned. Dad had fallen, and she couldn't lift him up off the floor. Luckily we are only a few minutes away, so my husband and I got in the car and went over to Mom and Dad's house. When we got there, Dad was on the floor, all right. He was wedged between the chair and the bathroom door. He looked so frail and helpless lying there. It had been a long time since I had seen my Dad in his underwear, and I was a little embarrassed. Luckily my husband was with me to pick Dad up and put him in the chair while I went into the other room to talk with my mom. Dad really didn't look very good, but Mom insisted that everything was O.K. and told us we should go home and not worry. So we went home and didn't worry. After all, Dad was eighty-one years old, and he probably had gotten up too fast and tripped. At least that's what we thought until the next call came. It was the following morning and Mom sounded very upset this time. Dad was on the floor again, and she needed help getting him up. My husband was at work, so I drove alone to Mom and Dad's house to see if I could pick him up. When I arrived, I found Dad on the floor by the bed. He looked terrible, and he was having a lot of difficulty breathing. When I tried to lift him, I couldn't move him, and he screamed in pain when I touched his left hip. I tried again to lift him, but he was too heavy, and I didn't want to hurt him or myself. I was scared to death, and Mom looked worse than I. The only thing left to do was dial 911 and ask for the fire department's paramedics. When they arrived, Dad was having a lot of difficulty breathing and was pale. His lips were bluish. The paramedics immobilized him and took him to the emergency room. After about two hours of examinations and tests, the emergency room doctor gave us the news. Dad had pneumonia and a broken hip. He would need to have surgery to fix the hip, but the pneumonia made the surgery even more risky than it normally would be. When the doctor asked how long Dad had not been feeling well, we really couldn't say for sure. We told the doctor that Dad had fallen the day before, but we really hadn't thought anything of it. The doctor explained to us that often when elderly people fall, it indicates the onset of a serious illness. In other words, Dad had fallen the day before because he was weak from the pneumonia that was slowly developing. If we had recognized that Dad fell because of the pneumonia, we probably could have prevented the second fall and the fractured hip. We also could have taken Dad to the hospital earlier to get treatment for the pneumonia. Dad recovered from this ordeal after about eight months, but he is not the same. He seems to have aged more in the last eight months than he had in the last five years. Had I only known then what I know now, perhaps we could have avoided this catastrophe.

Falls and fractures in the elderly are all too common and can have devastating results. There are many causes for falling in the elderly, and as caregivers it is our job to protect our loved ones and take a proactive stance in prevention. There are more than two hundred thousand hip fractures as a result of falls in this country every year. The emotional, physical and financial costs of hip fractures due to falls are astronomical. So what can we do? We can attempt to find potential causes for falls and offer treatment in order to preempt or prevent a falling episode. We can also work to treat osteoporosis, the devastating condition that causes our elderly loved ones to lose bone mass and fracture bones easily. Early treatment of osteoporosis may be beneficial; however, much of the bone loss has occurred by the time our parents are in their eighth and ninth decades of life. Bones are brittle, and fractures can occur with even the slightest movement or trauma. Because of the frailty of the skeletal bones, it is essential that we concentrate on how to prevent falls and accidents. The most common fractures due to the effects of osteoporosis are fractures of the hip, spinal vertebrae (compression fractures), wrists, arms and shoulders. Fractures in a frail eighty-year-old take longer to heal than fractures in a young, strong thirty-year-old. Often, fractures lead to immobility, which in turn leads to further disability. When an older person goes to bed or doesn't walk for even a week or two, the ability to walk can be substantially compromised. Keeping our elderly parents safely mobile is a prime objective of the caregiver.

If you are caring for an elderly parent in your home, or if you oversee the care in your parent's home, it would be wise to spend a few preventive hours now, educating yourself on preventing falls rather than sharing several painful months of rehabilitation at your parent's bedside.

We don't have to be medical detectives to see the potential for falls in the elderly. Just observe an elderly person walking, and you can readily see changes in gait, posture, balance and reaction time. When an elderly person loses her balance, it may be very difficult for her to right herself before a fall. Changes in vision, in hearing, and in the nervous system's ability to send and receive environmental stimuli can contribute to falls. If your elderly parent is having difficulty with walking, standing, or getting in and out of bed, a chair, or on and off the toilet, have a physician or physical therapist do an evaluation. The professional may be able to recommend walking aides and exercises that can improve balance and strength. Correcting vision can also be helpful in preventing falls, so be sure that eyes are checked regularly. Even wearing the proper shoes and having foot disorders treated can aid in preventing falls, so I recommend that a podiatrist (foot doctor) be consulted if walking becomes difficult. The results of Parkinson's disease, strokes, and arthritis can also contribute to falls. It is important that these illnesses be properly assessed and treated on an ongoing basis.

Falls can be the result of internal factors in the elderly person or external elements, such as hazards in the environment. In order to assist the physician in determining the cause of falling, it is important for the caregiver to gather information. Information that should be gathered includes: what your parent was doing immediately prior to the fall (standing up, turning, urinating); how your parent felt before the fall (dizzy, weak, numb); the time the falls are occurring; where the falls are occurring; the number of falls and your parent's subjective report of the fall (e.g., "I felt weak all of a sudden, and my legs buckled under me" or "I felt my heart beat very fast, and the next thing I knew I was on the floor").

Gathering this information will assist the physician in assessing potential causes and treatments for the fall. The caregiver should be aware that it is very common for the elderly to fall at the beginning of a medical illness. If an elderly person already has difficulty walking, an acute illness can be extra stress, which is sufficient to cause weakness, poor balance and falls. An occasional fall may be overlooked, but if your loved one had never fallen before and is now, suddenly, starting to fall, you should initiate a thorough examination by a physician. Infections are a major cause of illness in the elderly, and infections in the lungs and urinary tract may show up as confusion and falls, rather than fever. The opening story in this chapter illustrated how an unnoticed infection resulted in two falls and a fractured hip.

Dizziness from a drop in blood pressure when rising from a sitting or lying position can also lead to falls. Treatment of heart and circulatory problems can be initiated if such problems are contributing factors to the dizziness and falls. Another potential cause of falling that we can easily control is medications. Any time a fall occurs, you should check to see if a new medicine has been started or a current medicine has been changed or discontinued. Medicines to control blood pressure can cause drastic blood pressure drops, dizziness and falls. Medicines for pain or sleep can cause poor attention and drowsiness, and may lead to falls. Diuretics can cause dehydration and chemical imbalances in the body; these may also lead to falls. Any medicine taken at the wrong dosage or with an interacting medicine is a potential culprit. If in doubt when a fall occurs, check your parent's medications. Also be sure to have your parent's physician do a physical examination that includes blood work and an electrocardiogram. In addition, the physician may choose to do an electrocardiogram (heart monitoring) over a twenty-four-hour period to see if heart abnormalities are causing falls. An evaluation of medications with the physician is valuable and should be done regularly.

We depend so much on the medical profession to help in our assessment and treatment of falls, when in reality there are several things we, as lay caregivers, can do to prevent accidents from occurring. Common sense alterations of the physical environment can be done right away and at little or no cost. Take the time to go through your elderly parent's home to assess and correct safety hazards.

No matter how medically sophisticated we get in treating possible internal causes of falls, it does no good if a fall is caused by your parent's simply tripping. When young people trip they usually have the balance, speed and agility to right themselves before hitting the ground. Our elderly loved ones simply don't retain these abilities, and when they do fall their brittle bones may break very easily. To heal an eighty-year-old broken bone is much more difficult than removing the extension cord that was tripped over, causing the fracture. My advice is to be practical and spend some time looking around your elderly parent's home. Look from the ground up for accidents waiting to happen.

Remove clutter, electrical cords, low sitting tables, throw rugs without proper backing, furniture that has sharp protruding edges and any other potential dangers you can see. Ask your parent to walk around the house and observe any potential danger. To prevent slips, be sure that floors are not highly waxed. Stairs should be in good repair, and the staircase should be well illuminated at night. If necessary, put in brighter bulbs and make switches available at the top and bottom of the stairs. There should also be railing on both sides of the stairs, if possible, and I suggest identifying the first and last step with bright colors. Turn off the lights and walk around the house. See what you trip over or run into. Night lights should be available in case your parent gets up in the night to use the bathroom. Lights connected to motion detectors can also be helpful in case our loved one forgets to turn the light on when she gets up at night. Be sure that the light doesn't shine in the eyes because this may cause temporary blindness and disorientation.

In the bathroom, all tubs, showers and toilets should be fitted with grab bars and rails at the proper height. Non-skid mats or strips should be placed where there are possibilities of slips and falls. Ground fault interrupter plugs would also be a good idea to install around areas where electricity might come into contact with water. These plugs can be installed by an electrician and will automatically shut off the power to a socket should an electrical appliance fall into the water. Grab bars, raised toilet seats and other adaptive equipment can be purchased and installed by qualified home health and medical equipment companies. You can find their names in the phone book or associated with your local pharmacy.

It often helps to do something as simple as rearranging furniture, so that a clear path is created from the bed to the bathroom. Putting one side of the bed against the wall may also help in some cases, especially if exiting on the far side of the bed and walking around causes trips and falls. Check the height of the chairs. Can your loved one comfortably sit down and stand up from them? Arm rests on the chairs may also help her to get in and out of the chair safely.

When you walk through the house, look for raised thresholds or loose carpeting that can be potential hazards. Any potential bump or dip should be corrected. Throw rugs without proper backing should be removed. Be sure everything in the house is within reach, including food on the shelves. Reaching or standing on unstable chairs or stools can cause loss of balance and falls. Leave familiar items in familiar places, and instruct cleaning people to do the same. Do your safety inspections regularly. It may be life saving.

Safety in the home is not limited to the prevention of falls. The home should be secured from intruders, and help should be accessible if needed. If your parent is visually or hearing impaired, you will want to get a special phone that has large number buttons and amplifiers on the earpiece. The phone is a lifeline to the outside world and should be accessible and easy to use. Important phone numbers of relatives, doctors, fire department and police should be posted by each phone in very large print, to allow quick and easy access in an emergency. Speed dial phones can be programmed with important phone numbers for hurried use.

If possible, you should arrange for neighbors or postal carriers to check on your loved one if she is not seen or if the mail or newspaper is not being picked up. Most people are friendly and would be glad to assist you if asked. In some communities there are emergency alert response systems available through local hospitals and agencies. These allow the elderly person to wear a portable communication unit at all times. Should an emergency arise, she simply pushes a button on the unit that activates at a local monitoring station. The monitoring station will in turn summon help. If available and affordable, this may bring peace of mind to both you and your parent.

During your regular home safety visits, check the cabinets for dangerous chemicals that may accidentally be ingested, mixed or ignited. Chemicals that are flammable should not be stored near the water heater or open flames. I recommend removing all dangerous chemicals to avoid accidental ignition or ingestion. Check the medicine cabinets to see that medication is being properly stored and labeled. Expired medications should be discarded to avoid confusion.

Older people can easily be scalded by hot water because of decreased sensation of the skin or because of slow reaction time. A fall in the bathtub with hot water running can be deadly, especially if your parent can't reach to turn off the water. Hot water temperature should be regulated so that it doesn't exceed 110 degrees.

Picture windows and sliding doors should have stickers placed on them to keep an elderly person from inadvertently walking through the glass.

Fire safety is of utmost importance in an elderly person's home. Memory problems, along with a diminished ability to evacuate in an emergency fire situation, make fire safety a must. Smoke detectors should be placed throughout the home, especially in the kitchen area. It is not uncommon for a memory-impaired elderly person to leave a pot cooking on the stove and forget about it. Your local fire department would be more than happy to assist you by inspecting your parent's home and making recommendations. Portable space heaters should be removed, and smoking should be discouraged. If your elderly parent is very frail and insists on smoking, be sure to have her wear a fire resistant apron. These aprons prevent ashes dropped on clothing from igniting and catching the person on fire. I have purchased these types of aprons for my nursing home patients who insist on smoking. The aprons, however, are hard to find. Perhaps your local nursing home can tell you where to buy one; your local fire department may have some recommendations. Many older people also use oxygen in the home. If your parent uses oxygen, be sure that it is stored and handled safely. Get instructions from the oxygen supplier on how to prevent fires and explosions. I recommend oxygen concentrator machines for long term use, since they are much safer than the tanks. Gas stoves can also be a danger. Gas can be left on by mistake and asphyxiation can result. Be sure that knobs are clearly marked in large print to indicate the on and off positions. If you don't trust your elderly parent's judgment, you may wish to consider disabling the gas stove if cooking is no longer done anyway. Check with your gas company for recommendations.

Many elderly people fall victim to violent crime, theft and larceny. Criminals view older people as prime victims. Loneliness can cause your elderly parent to befriend a dishonest person who may take advantage of her. If your parent mentions any new strangers or friends around, be sure to investigate the people. The same goes for salespeople who may want to sell insurance or home improvements. If your elderly parent has an answering machine, you or your spouse should record the message so that the caller won't know that an elderly person lives alone in the house. Be especially vigilant each month at the time when social security or pension checks are received in the mail. If possible, have these checks directly deposited into the bank. If you are really concerned, ask your elderly parent to add your signature to her checking or savings account. Print on the checks a line for two signatures, and state on the checks that two signatures are required. If this is too intrusive, you can leave it as a one signature account; if that option is taken, you should be sure that there is no substantial amount of money in it.

The house can be secured with dead bolt locks, and it should be well lit from the outside at night. A dog or alarm system is also helpful in deterring crime. The police department can be of assistance in securing your parent's home against criminals, so I would ask for their help.

Safety outside the home is just as important as safety inside the home. Outside areas should also be evaluated for hazards that may cause falls. Look for raised areas or potholes in the walkways, and make sure these areas are corrected. Be sure that porches and stairs are well lit and that the top and bottom stairs are painted yellow or white. Because stepping off a curb can result in a fall, it is wise to pull up to the driveway when getting Mom or Dad in and out of the car. If you live in weather where rain and snow may create hazardous walking conditions, be very cautious about assisting Mom or Dad at these times. Garage areas and back yards should also be assessed for safety, especially if hobbies and activities are carried out in these areas.

I don't want to turn you into a worried adult child of an aging parent, but the prevention of injuries is a prime role of the caregiver. Parents childproof their homes in order to prevent their children from accidental poisoning, drowning, electrocution, falls, burns and other avoidable catastrophes. As a caregiver, you need to use your judgment about how much help and intervention your elderly parent may need. By no means should you treat your parent like a child and tell her whom to associate with and what to do. Merely take a preventive, deterrent stance when it comes to home safety and security, for the welfare of your elderly parent.

5

DEALING WITH DEPRESSION

A VERY COMMON PROBLEM among the elderly is depression, a condition which is often undetected and untreated. Contributing to depression are such factors as loneliness, poor health, financial worries, death of loved ones and friends, loss of self-esteem, boredom, lack of purpose and goals, the thought of death and dependency, and a myriad of physiological changes and conditions.

Everyone feels bad occasionally and may even complain of being sad or depressed. These feelings are normal and usually go away without the need for professional help or intervention. People bounce back, adjust their life's course and get back to normal. Unfortunately, many elderly do not have the resilience to bounce back, especially if their depression is being caused by unpleasant circumstances over which they have no control.

Depression may present itself in many ways. An elderly person may express feelings of sadness, helplessness, and hopelessness over a period of weeks or months. The depressed person may feel that she is of no worth to anyone, or she may say that she is just tired of living. In addition to the emotional complaints accompanying depression, physical symptoms are often present: poor appetite, weight loss, complaints about bowel function, difficulty sleeping, loss of energy, fatigue, tearfulness, complaints of pain, difficulty concentrating, agitation. Any of these symptoms, alone or in combination, indicate the possibility of depression.

The importance of recognizing the signs of depression in your loved one cannot be overemphasized, because if left untreated, the results can be deadly. **Suicide in the elderly is more common than most people think, and it is often a result of depression.** Generally, when elderly people attempt suicide, the outcome is very lethal and frequently successful. They simply feel that there is no hope left, and they want to die. They are not merely crying out for help, nor do they generally attempt suicide to manipulate others. A depressed elderly person may see suicide as a viable alternative to a life of intractable pain and suffering. Suicide in the elderly is usually underreported or not suspected. Family members and health professionals may think the elderly person died of natural causes, when in reality he or she purposely took an overdose of medications.

Because of the correlation between depression and suicide, be careful to notice signs before it is too late. If your elderly loved one expresses the wish to die, explore these feelings. Are they natural feelings that many elderly people feel, or are these feelings suicidal in nature and due to depression? Seek the assistance of your elderly parent's physician or a counselor who is skilled in working with the elderly. If your parent says she is going to kill herself, take her seriously. Find out if she has a plan of how or when she is going to take her life. Be aware that elderly people may kill themselves with the pills that were prescribed to treat their depression. This is one reason why only small supplies should be prescribed at a time. Another reason is that your parent has to go back for refills and checkups, and thus remains connected to the doctor. Even if your parent doesn't specifically say that she plans to commit suicide, be aware of subtle signs. If she was depressed and is now suddenly happy, this may be a sign that the decision to end pain and suffering via suicide has been made. If she seems to be concentrating on what she wants to leave to relatives upon her death, you may want to be extra vigilant. Be aware that after the death of a spouse or after being diagnosed with a devastating illness, depression and suicidal thoughts may surface. If any question exists in your mind, seek professional help.

Her name is Dorothy. At eighty-two she recalls how each year has brought both joy and sorrow. She has had a good life compared to most, she explains—a marriage of fifty-one years, children, grandchildren, the comforts of a nice home and good friends. Yes, the Lord has kept a watchful eye on Dorothy, and she feels that soon He will be calling her to join Him. She explains that there is just nothing left for her to live for, especially since her husband died a year ago. Dorothy and her husband were inseparable. Fifty-one years of marriage cannot easily be forgotten. Dorothy's children have noticed a difference in her over the past few months, even though Dorothy denies that anything is wrong. She is just not herself anymore according to her daughters. When the children call or visit, Dorothy just tells them that she is tired and doesn't feel up to the commotion.

Dorothy has also grown increasingly homebound. She no longer goes out visiting or shopping with friends. In the past, Dorothy was an impeccable dresser. She was never seen without a dress, make-up and her hair fixed. These last few months, however, Dorothy doesn't bother to change out of her housecoat. She rarely does her hair anymore and is now even neglecting personal hygiene. Each time her children visit, they notice that she is losing weight. When they check the refrigerator, they see food that is spoiled and left over from their last visit. When questioned, Dorothy just says that she has no appetite or interest in food. Nothing tastes good anymore, and besides, why should she bother fixing anything if there is nobody to eat with anymore. Each visit for the family is becoming increasingly alarming and frustrating. They ask Dorothy how she feels, and she responds the same way every time, "Oh, I'm miserable. My stomach hurts. I'm having trouble with my bowels. I wake up at night and can't fall back to sleep. My bones ache and I just don't feel like getting out of bed anymore." In fact, on several visits, Dorothy's children would find Dorothy still in bed at three in the afternoon.

Dorothy is deteriorating in front of everyone's eyes, and the whole family feels helpless. When they called the family doctor, much to their dismay, he told them that they should expect this type of deterioration in someone who is eighty-two years old. He offered to prescribe some sleeping pills to help Dorothy sleep and said that he would prescribe some medicine to settle her stomach and bowels if they wanted. He couldn't make a house call, however, and Dorothy insisted that she wasn't up to going to see the doctor.

The family isn't satisfied, but they don't know where to turn for help. One daughter suggested that Dorothy come stay with her for a while, but the daughter's husband quickly said, "Absolutely not." The family thought about a nursing home and immediately decided that this option would make Mom worse and lead to a more rapid decline. Nobody knows what to do, but it is becoming increasingly more obvious that something has to be done right away.

This scenario illustrates a common plight of children who are caring for aging parents. Family members see changes in a parent, but they can't identify what specifically is wrong. It is very difficult to be around a loved one who is depressed and complaining all the time. Many times just the negative behavior of the depressed elderly person furthers her isolation, because nobody wants to be around her to hear about her problems. Caregivers understand a fractured hip, a stroke or cancer. You can see the concrete results of these problems, and you feel that your parent wasn't responsible for the condition. When the caregiver deals with a depressed elderly parent, the problem is more difficult to understand and empathize with. You may believe that your parent is being weak or manipulative. You may want her to just snap out of it, when in reality she cannot.

The importance of family communication and planning is underscored by its being discussed in several chapters of this book. It is an absolute necessity. In the best of situations, the family communicates well, and every family member has the same agenda. The agenda, of course, is to develop a plan that will help the elderly parent and relieve the family of stress. In the worst of situations the family doesn't agree on anything, doesn't care what happens to Mom or Dad, and/or doesn't have the knowledge, fortitude or motivation to offer effective assistance. Dynamics within families are very complicated; this is especially true with family problems involving elderly parents. Relationships with elderly parents have had decades to develop or decline. Many children simply do not know how to offer care to an aging parent because of the role reversal. After all, we are taught from birth to listen to our parents and follow their advice. Some elderly parents find this change in roles difficult to accept, and they are extremely resistant to suggestions and change, unless they are involved in the decision making process. Dorothy was resistant to getting help. Her depression caused her to isolate herself, but her children were not going to let that happen. They took the first step in properly caring for their mother by realizing that there was a problem. They observed their mother acting and looking *different*. They may not have recognized the cause of the problem as depression, but they knew enough to intervene and ask for professional assistance. Unfortunately in the case of Dorothy, the necessary professional intervention was not offered when it was requested from the doctor. The doctor attributed Dorothy's problems and complaints to old age. As caregivers you should not give up or accept this "old age" answer.

You may be dealing with depression if your elderly loved one suffers from symptoms such as these: sad mood, anxiety, agitation, difficulty sleeping, poor appetite (with or without weight loss), feelings of hopelessness, decreased self-care motivation, declines in basic activities (such as dressing, bathing, and walking), difficulty concentrating or even complaints of memory loss, constipation and diarrhea. Not all of these symptoms need to be present, and each elderly person suffering from depression is different. If you are not sure, seek the help of a professional psychiatrist, social worker, or therapist who is experienced in treating mental health problems in the elderly.

Psychiatric services are notoriously underutilized in the elderly population. Why? Perhaps it is because of the stigma associated with mental health care in the distant past; perhaps it is due to symptoms which are mistakenly being attributed to old age. Some people think that the elderly are resistant and rigid in their belief systems and that counseling cannot lead to positive change. I disagree with that theory. On the contrary, elderly people are survivors; they have many years of accumulated life experience upon which they can call.

If you suspect depression in your elderly parent, you should assist her in receiving a comprehensive evaluation.

In some instances depression can be caused by physiological abnormalities, so proper laboratory blood work and physical examination are important. A competent physician should perform the examination. Either a psychiatrist, internist, or family practitioner with experience in geriatrics would be sufficient to perform the examination. Some medications which your parent takes may also contribute to depression, so be sure that a thorough medication evaluation is undertaken at the time of the physical exam.

Some depressions are biological in nature and caused by abnormal chemical balances in the body and brain. Some depressions are the result of reactions to circumstances of life. Many depressions are caused by a combination of biological and life circumstances. Even if an exact cause of the depression cannot be determined, appropriate therapy should be initiated.

Counseling can help an elderly person, but counseling in the absence of environmental changes may not be as beneficial. Talking about feelings of loneliness, guilt, anger and despair is helpful, and merely developing a trusting relationship with a therapist is therapeutic. If you sit down and list the problems your elderly parent experiences at any one time, you may then understand why she is depressed. If chronic pain contributes to the depression, then steps should be taken to offer pain control interventions. If your elderly parent is having difficulty with hearing or eyesight, perhaps correction of these factors will have an impact on depression. If your parent used to be able to read, watch television, sew, or enjoy any other activity, your assisting her in participating again might be helpful. Ask your parent what she enjoys doing the most. It may simply be a visit with the grandchildren; if that's so, perhaps visits can be stepped up. Loneliness and lack of purpose often can contribute to depression. If you didn't have a purpose or person to wake up to every day, you also might become depressed fairly rapidly. It may seem silly, but a pet can be very good medicine. A dog, cat or bird can reintroduce life in the house and give your parent something to care for. Spiritual counseling or intervention by clergy might bring hope to your parent. Try to focus on the positive while allowing your parent to share her concerns with you during your visits. If therapy is undertaken, find out if you can participate. There may be issues with the children that your parent needs to resolve and get closure on.

If the doctor recommends an antidepressant medication, be sure to learn about how the medicine should work. The medication the doctor chooses should be one that is well tolerated in the elderly and one that has the fewest side effects. The doctor needs to take into account the medical problems your parent suffers from as well as what other medications she is currently taking. The doctor may want to start the medication slowly at low doses, and the medication should be monitored at least monthly. Some medications for depression may take several weeks to work, so be sure that your parent doesn't stop taking the medicine prematurely. Also, be sure that she is taking the medication properly; if not taken correctly, antidepressant medications can be harmful.

A large proportion of the elderly people with whom I have worked are searching desperately for a purpose. This lack of purpose brings despair and depression. Because they have nothing to do each morning when they arise, they just sit and worry and become depressed. When you give an elderly, depressed person suggestions about what to do, you often get responses such as, "I can't do that anymore because I can't see," or "I don't have the strength," or "My hands don't work," or "That doesn't interest me."

It takes tremendous energy on the caregiver's part to motivate an elderly parent who is depressed. Don't try to do it all at once, and don't expect a dramatic change in your parent overnight. Introduce a small idea on which you know your elderly parent is able to follow through. Upon completion of a task, be sure to give plenty of encouragement. Elderly people need to be needed, but often they are thrust into dependent positions in which they are the ones receiving. Don't be afraid to assign some responsibility, and be sure to let your parent know that you still need her for advice and comfort. I have been surprised when elderly patients of mine have been extremely depressed and hopeless until one of their adult children became sick and needed them. They will do anything to get out of bed and help console their children. The focus shifts from the elderly person's needs to the needs of the adult child, and boy, what a difference! I'm not suggesting that you pretend you are sick and needy. Merely let Mom be mom again, and occasionally ask for advice.

Sometimes a change of environment is also helpful when you are trying to intervene with an elderly parent suffering from depression. If Mom is isolated in a large, cold house, perhaps a move to a more cheerful therapeutic environment would help. Don't make the decision about where is the best place for Mom to live. Ask your elderly parent and provide options. The more your parent is involved in the decisions about living arrangements, the better the results may be. Just remember that your world and reality may be different than your eighty-year-old parent's.

Dates to look forward to often help with adding reason and purpose to one's life. If your parent is depressed, it may help if you try to get her more engaged by assisting in planning events for the future. The wedding coming up or the expected birth of a grandchild may be just the thing to look forward to. If you feel that nothing else is helping, just being there to listen and love may be all that you can do. Depression is a serious problem, so don't try to do it alone. Get help as soon as you recognize the symptoms in your aging parent. The sooner the intervention, the less likely it is that the depression will have long lasting effects.

6

MONITORING THE USE OF MEDICATIONS

I knew something was wrong with Mom when I called her on the phone today. At first she didn't recognize who I was, and she didn't seem to be making a whole lot of sense. She could hardly follow the conversation. In the middle of a sentence she told me that she had to get dressed for the opera, and then she hung up. Mom had never gone to the opera, and she certainly was not going at eight o'clock in the morning. Something was definitely wrong, so once again I took the morning off from work and headed to her house. When I arrived, Mom was totally confused and hallucinating. I had no idea what was wrong; I was hoping that Mom hadn't had a stroke or something. I figured that I would get her dressed and take her to the hospital before things got worse. I went into the bedroom to look for some clothes for Mom, and I saw on the dresser about five bottles of pills. I also looked into the bathroom and found another three bottles. I looked in Mom's purse and found two more bottles, and—lo and behold—in the kitchen, there was yet another bottle of pills.

At this point, even as a lay person, I realized that these medications might have had something to do with the way Mom was acting. I asked her how many of what pills she had taken, and she had no idea what I was talking about. I decided to throw these twelve bottles of pills into a paper bag and let the doctors sort them out. When we got to the hospital, the doctor reviewed the pills for me. Apparently they had been prescribed by three different doctors. None of the doctors knew what the other two were prescribing, and Mom was taking two of the same kind of pills for the same condition. For her heart, she was taking Lasix® (a brand name) prescribed by one doctor and its generic form, furosemide, prescribed by another doctor. She was getting the same drug at twice the required dosage. Apparently, she was supposed to be taking potassium also, but she didn't take it because she said it upset her stomach. She had three different pain pills, two different pills for her blood pressure, some pills for anxiety and sleep and even a pill for depression. After some blood work, it was discovered that Mom was dehydrated and had a dangerously low level of potassium. Luckily, after a few days in the hospital, her mental state cleared up and she was back to herself again. I had no idea that Mom was taking so many medications. We have it all straightened out now, and I'm insisting that Mom sees only one doctor. The doctor said that Mom would have died if I had not been around. The cause of death would have been her not understanding the label on a prescription bottle.

In my day-to-day care of the elderly, I have become extremely aware of the problems that medications can cause. Medications that are intended to help, often make things worse, if they aren't taken properly. It is unfortunate that medications are sometimes used to find easy solutions to very complicated issues. If an elderly person is anxious, it is easier for a doctor to prescribe a pill for anxiety than to sit down for an hour and explore what is the basis for the anxiety. If someone is depressed after the death of a loved one, an antidepressant medication may be prescribed instead of an offer of grief counseling. Once prescribed, the effectiveness or necessity of the medication may never be evaluated, and the person may take these pills for life. Any medications, even if prescribed and taken properly, can cause serious side effects and consequences in an elderly, debilitated person. It may sound silly, but the best medicine in the world for an elderly person can simply be the touch of a warm hand, the compassion of a listening ear, the interest of another human being, and a feeling of hope that life will improve and be O.K. again.

As caregivers, we need to be acutely aware of the potential problems associated with medications. Many elderly people take between four to ten medications a day. Often these medicines are prescribed by different physicians in an uncoordinated manner and at higher than therapeutic doses for an elderly patient. Problems with memory or difficulty understanding medication instructions also may contribute to negative effects of medications.

Looking at the matter simply, an elderly person's reactions to a drug may be different than a younger person's, due to physiological, age related changes in drug absorption, drug distribution, and drug clearance or elimination. In other words, a medication taken by an elderly person may take longer to be absorbed, may not be distributed in the body tissues effectively, and may stay in the body for a longer period of time. Young, healthy adults may be able to tolerate higher doses of medications due to their better general health and physiological function. Also, many of the recommended drug dispensing guidelines may not be applicable to the elderly because the directions are based on data measured from young, healthy subjects. An elderly person with multiple, chronic, medical problems and decreased body function will not require the same amount of medications as a 180-pound 25-year-old truck driver.

As caregivers and advocates for our elderly parents, we need to be cautious and prudent in monitoring medications. The importance of choosing and maintaining a good relationship with one physician cannot be overstated in this area. To reduce the risk of medication problems, be sure that before any medication is prescribed, there is a clear reason for taking it. There should be a current diagnosis for every medicine taken, and the diagnoses and continued need for the medication should be evaluated regularly. After treatment is completed, all remaining medication should be discarded to avoid future confusion or self-diagnosis and treatment. I recommend that a caregiver take all medicines in the house—including over-the-counter medications—to the physician's office at each office visit. Each medication should be reviewed to see if it is helping, if there are any side effects, and if it is still necessary. As a general rule, the fewer the medications taken the better your loved one will be.

Make sure to assist your parent in giving the physician a careful drug history. Keep track of any previous medications taken and any side effects experienced. Don't be afraid to ask questions and offer suggestions. You should ask the doctor to explain potential side effects of any new drugs and ask for justification for its use. Ask about proper doses, prescribing times, and possible interactions with other medications. As a general rule, in prescribing for the elderly, the lowest possible dose of a medication should be prescribed, and it should be gradually increased until the therapeutic results are achieved.

If the physician is not cooperative in explaining the medication program, ask the dispensing pharmacist for help or find a physician who is willing to take the time to work with you. These same principles of medication monitoring apply if your parent is in a nursing home or retirement facility and is having medications managed by the facility staff. Don't assume that medications managed by the facility are being prescribed and given properly, just because someone else is involved. Commonly, in nursing homes or other facilities, a medication may be prescribed over the phone for a minor problem and be continued without regard to duration of therapy and other medications being taken. This may also be the case in a hospital or nursing home if a medicine is prescribed by the on-call physician rather than the attending physician, who actually knows the patient. It is wise, therefore, to assist your parent in medication monitoring, even outside the realm of the home caregiving environment. If approached in a positive, friendly manner, most health care professionals would be happy to explore and share medication information with you and your loved one.

Since the beginning of time, man has been searching for the fountain of youth. A miracle potion or elixir to prevent or reverse the effects of aging has yet to be discovered, and it is doubtful that man will ever be able to rewrite such a strong natural law of nature as aging.

While we may never discover the fountain of youth, there is no reason to needlessly suffer the ills of old age if proper interventions with medications is available. Older people often suffer from multiple, chronic illnesses that won't be cured by medications, but may be effectively managed.

Even the best medications, prescribed properly, are useless or even dangerous if not taken properly. There are many ways that medications can be taken improperly by an elderly person. Medicine doses may be forgotten; they may be taken at the wrong dosages and times; they may be taken without necessary precautions; they may be taken for too long or short a period of time; or a wrong medication may be taken in error. Many elderly people do not take their medications simply because they cannot afford to purchase them or because they are unable to get transportation to a pharmacy. Physical barriers that may prevent an elderly person from taking medication properly include the inability to open the container because of arthritis, the inability to hold and swallow a pill, and the inability to see the prescription label or pills.

As caregivers we need to educate ourselves on all medicines given to our elderly loved ones, and we should monitor medication dispensing and compliance as closely as possible. Remember to ask the prescribing physician everything about the medicine and the reason for taking the drug. The fewer the medications and the simpler the instructions and administration times, the better the results will be.

I recommend that caregivers carefully document the medications taken by their elderly parents and that they create simple instructions according to the the eight-step format outlined below. The physician or pharmacist is instrumental in providing this information; I suggest that you make up a sheet for each medicine prescribed and bring all of them to the doctor or pharmacist for help in completing the information. These medication information sheets should be in large print. The name and phone number of the doctor and pharmacist should also be written down in case any questions arise. I recommend leaving all of this information by the phone or in a central location in the house, so that emergency personnel can locate it in a medical emergency. Information should include:

1. LOCATION OF MEDICATION, e.g., in the medicine chest, on the kitchen counter

2. PROPER STORAGE, e.g., in the refrigerator, in original container; in dark bottle, in pill dispensing box

3. NAME OF MEDICATION, BOTH PRODUCT AND CHEMICAL, WITH DOSE, e.g., Valium® 5 mg (diazepam), Restoril® 15 mg (temazapam). By naming the brand name and the chemical name, you can check to see that two medications of the same type are not being taken simultaneously, by mistake.

4. WHAT THE MEDICATION IS FOR, e.g., heart, arthritis, sleep, pain, blood pressure

5. DESCRIPTION OF THE PILL, e.g., 1/2 white, 1/2 red capsule; small blue tablet; large white tablet

6. MEDICATION INSTRUCTIONS, e.g., take one tablet at breakfast and dinner; take one capsule every six hours; place one tablet under your tongue for chest pain and call physician if pain does not go away in fifteen minutes

7. DURATION OF THERAPY, e.g., take until medicine is finished; take until next office visit in three weeks

8. POSSIBLE SIDE EFFECTS AND PRECAUTIONS, e.g., poor appetite, diarrhea, increase in confusion, irregular heart rate, urinary retention, irritability; do not take with alcohol; take while sitting to avoid dizziness. Call the doctor if these symptoms develop.

It may be difficult as a caregiver to determine whether your loved one can safely take her own medications. We do not want to take away independence or autonomy from our elderly parent, but in the case of medication administration, sometimes it is better to be safe than sorry. If you visit your parent regularly, it may be wise to check each medicine bottle and make sure that medicine is being taken properly. Ask your parent how often she is taking which pill and if there have been any side effects. When I'm not sure of proper self-administration, I will count pills and tally the count against the date the prescription was issued. In other words, if a medicine was prescribed on the first of the month at a dose of three pills a day, on the fifteenth of the month there should be forty-five pills fewer than the original number prescribed. If there are sixty pills missing or twenty-five pills missing, you can be sure that too much or too little medication is being taken.

Many drugs are prescribed for the elderly on an as-needed basis, or what professionals term (PRN basis). Drugs prescribed on an as-needed basis may be for pain, sleeplessness or even anxiety. Check with your loved one to see how much of the as-needed medication is being used. If your loved one is taking a pill for anxiety that was prescribed on an as-needed basis, there may be a question as to what determines the need. Does she take the pill when she is a little anxious or very anxious? How does she subjectively describe anxiety? What is causing the anxiety and is it treatable by something other than medication? What is the potential for overdosage if the prescription says to take one pill as needed for anxiety and doesn't give the maximum number of pills that can be safely taken in a twenty-four hour period? Depending on your elderly loved one's judgment, prescriptions given on an as-needed basis can lead to problems. I have seen sleep medications prescribed on an as-needed basis to elderly people who may take a pill at 7:00 p.m. to help them fall asleep by 8:00 p.m. If they don't fall asleep by 8:00, they take another pill. If they wake up at 2:00 a.m. and can't fall back to sleep, they take another pill. By the next day they are confused and unable to be aroused. If a sleeping pill is absolutely necessary, it should be given at the correct dose for an elderly person, prescribed at a set amount over a period of time, and used for a limited duration. Just to be safe, try to limit the number of medications prescribed on an as-needed basis. If as-needed medications are prescribed, the caregiver should carefully monitor their need and usage.

Be aware that medications which are used to help your elderly loved one may actually cause harm if not prescribed, taken, and monitored properly. To prevent potential problems, keep the following key concepts in mind.

- Utilize as few physicians as possible when getting prescriptions. If possible, have only one doctor issue prescriptions. If a doctor refers your parent to a specialist who prescribes a medication, be sure that it does not conflict with other prescribed medications.

- Bring all medications that are being taken to the physician at each visit. Include over-the-counter medications. Make sure that each medication which is being taken has a specific diagnosis or reason for administration. Ask the doctor what each medicine is for and what potential side effects are. Ask at each visit if the medicine currently being taken is still necessary, and find out why this is so. Ask if a blood level of a drug should be monitored—as could be necessary with the use of such drugs as digoxin, thyroid, Dilantin® or Coumadin®.

- Keep medications in a central location in the house, and keep a sheet as described earlier in this chapter on each medicine. Be sure that instructions are specific and understandable.

- Become educated on medicine. There are many books written for the lay public describing the effects of medications. The more you know about the medicine, the safer the medicine is, because you will recognize potential problems such as side effects, allergic reactions or overdose in your loved one.

- Always ask questions of the physician who prescribes medications. Doses of medications may be different for the elderly, and some medications should be completely avoided in the elderly. Many medications interact, resulting either in making one medicine more potent or in reducing the potency of one or both medicines.

- Don't be too quick to ask the doctor for medicine to cure an elderly parent's problem. On the other hand, while there may be conditions that we cannot cure, sometimes there are medications which, when properly taken, can help improve the quality of life. Don't forget the lifestyle factors that may influence the disease and aging process. Perhaps medication could be reduced if changes in lifestyle were made. The prescription for sleeping pills may not be necessary if your elderly parent is active, and not napping, during the day. Ask about alternatives to medications.

- Know what is being taken and why. As parents, we would not give our baby an adult medication at an adult dose. As children of elderly parents, we might be wise to keep the same idea in mind. What is good medicine for a strong, healthy adult may not be so good for a frail, chronically ill parent.

7

CARING FOR YOUR LOVED ONE AT HOME

Mrs. Katz is the normal, everyday, run-of-the-mill, American woman in her mid-eighties. She lives alone in a one-bedroom apartment that she has occupied for the last fifteen years, since her husband died. Mrs. Katz has three grown children—two sons who live in different states and a daughter who lives about forty minutes away by car.

Mrs. Katz has always been fiercely independent. She grew up in a time when you did for yourself in order to survive. Lately, however, Mrs. Katz has grown to be more reliant on her daughter for basic activities, such as shopping, paying bills, cleaning the house, transportation to and from the doctor, and sorting out instructions for medical care. Associated with this new dependence has come resentment from Mrs. Katz's daughter. She knows that her mom needs help, especially since her health has declined recently. What the daughter is struggling with is knowing what kind of help to give, how much and when to intervene, and where to get needed services.

She has considered moving her mom to a retirement hotel, but she knows that her mother would not go for this idea. Everything Mom knows and owns is comfortably placed in the one-bedroom apartment she has lived in for so long. Mom is quite alert and knows exactly where everything in the apartment is located. To move her would just create unnecessary discomfort. The daughter has tried to bring in help for Mom, but everyone she brings in, Mom kicks out. It appears that nobody does things for Mom like this loving daughter does.

Let's talk for a moment about this loving daughter. She is fifty-four years old and has been married for thirty years to the same man. They have three children—one in college and two teenagers at home. Her husband, a local businessman, has had a good job for the past ten years. He has had to curtail his work recently, however, because of a heart attack and recurrent chest pain. Financially, this family is just getting by, and the husband and wife are seriously concerned about how to prepare for their own retirement years.

Grandma Katz, when she was younger, fit in quite well with the family. When she was younger, she enjoyed baby-sitting and helping out with her grandchildren. The extra help during this time in the family's evolution allowed Mrs. Katz's daughter to go back to work and earn college money for the kids.

Currently this family system is experiencing significant stress, because of the increased demand Grandmother is placing on it. The daughter is becoming distraught, as she cares for her husband, children, and increasingly dependent mother.

This daughter has no time for herself, and she feels like a slave to everyone. She becomes impatient with Mom, angry at her husband and children, and guilty about not being able to do everything for everyone.

This guilt leads her to wonder whether she should ask Mom to move in with the family. By the time she comes to see me, she is a nervous wreck and hesitant to ask me the one million dollar question. She comes in, sits down stoically, takes a deep breath and seeks my counsel. We meet several times and I help her to set boundaries, have realistic expectations and find necessary help.

What is it that I have called the "million dollar question?" The million dollar question that adult children ask me, as a professional, is: "Should I take Mom home to live with me?" My answer isn't always worth a million dollars, but I do my best to help the whole family explore care options. It often seems to me that when adult children—usually daughters or daughters-in-law—ask me this question, they are hoping that I advise against taking a parent into their home. Many adult children feel obligated to care for a parent in their home, even if it is not advisable. Guilt and fear of what others will think about their not fulfilling an unspoken obligation often motivates these children's decisions.

The two million dollar question that is often asked of me is asked by the elderly parent. Guess what the question is? You are correct if you guessed that the question is: "Should I live with my daughter in her home?" Many dependent, elderly parents do not want to be a burden on the children. Even if they want to go live with a son or daughter, they may not let their feelings be known. Still others expect to move in with an adult child if the need arises, and they would think of no other living arrangements.

If your parent is having difficulty managing in her own home, it may be wise to investigate ways of bringing in home support services, prior to moving her in with you. A move at any age is difficult, because people get used to routines and familiar surroundings. This may be especially true with an elderly person who has some disability. It is not uncommon for an elderly, disabled person to have her home set up exactly the way she needs it to allow her to function on a day-to-day basis. Furniture may be strategically placed to guide her in walking throughout the house. Things she needs and uses may be within her reach. Schedules of daily activities may be currently arranged to her satisfaction. If Mom is happy and safe in her own home, maybe it is wise to let her stay there and bring services to her. If it is not practical or possible to bring services into your parent's home, then perhaps having a parent come live with you would be necessary. Think long and hard before making the commitment to bring a parent into your home. I recommend that the family sit down and discuss the pros and cons; the parent should be included in these discussions.

Caring for an elderly loved one in your home is a tremendous challenge, due to the many physical, financial, and emotional needs that may exist. Your ability to provide adequate care may be restricted by physical barriers in your home, such as stairs, lack of space, or inaccessible bathrooms. In addition, it may be quite difficult for you to supervise your parent during the day while you are away at work or at night when you are trying to sleep. Finding affordable, trustworthy help who will come to your home is also a problem for many caregivers.

Before bringing your parent to live with you, it is important to understand just how much care and what type of care will be necessary. Once the type and amount of care is established, you need to measure what resources are available in the home to meet the demand for services. Some caregivers tend to overestimate their own abilities, as well as the abilities and expected support of family and friends. Family and friends may offer to assist in the care of a parent, parent-in-law, or grandparent, until they see what it is really all about. Be very honest with yourself and your family if an elderly, dependent parent may be moving in. Everyone's comfort and safety has to be considered before accepting the responsibility of caring for an elderly loved one in the home. The feelings and needs of the caregiver's immediate family should be carefully evaluated and weighed. If family life is already stressful, and if you do not have everyone's support, the addition of a dependent parent into your home may have a negative impact on the entire family unit.

Before moving your parent in with you, sit down with the

whole family and have a meeting to talk everything through. I would include your elderly parent in this meeting if she/he is able to participate. You need to have accurate information to share with the family about what can be expected. Your parent's physicians, therapists, social workers or nurses can help develop a plan of care in the home by assisting you to answer the following questions.

How is Mom walking? Does she need a walker? Can she safely walk without assistance, or will she fall? Is the home safe for her to walk around in, or can she trip on obstacles? (See Chapter 4.) If Mom needs a wheelchair, are the bathrooms and halls accessible? If the home has stairs, can Mom negotiate them? Can she get on and off a chair or in and out of bed independently? Is there someone strong enough available to assist if Mom can't get on and off the bed, chair or toilet without assistance? What time of day or night is this assistance available? Is it safe to leave Mom alone in the house? If so, for how long can she be left alone? If Mom has memory loss, what are the dangers of her being left alone (e.g., in case of fire or her wandering away)? Is there someone reliable who can stay with Mom if the family is not at home? What is the cost and availability of the person? Can you bring your mom with you when you leave the house, or does her frailty and decreased mobility make it difficult? Can she get in and out of your car? Can a wheelchair fit in the car? Can Mom get dressed and undressed without assistance? If not, how much assistance does she require? Is there someone available to assist her with dressing and undressing? Can Mom bathe without assistance? If not, how much assistance does she need? Can she get in and out of the home's shower or tub? Are there grab bars or shower chairs? Is there someone strong enough at home to assist her in showering and bathing? If not, is someone available to come in on a regular basis to assist? How much will this cost? Does Mom need assistance with preparing meals or eating? If so, is someone available to prepare and serve at least three meals a day? If she needs a special diet, is it available? Can Mom take her own medications? If not, is someone available to administer the medications correctly at the right times? Is Mom able to control her urine or bowel functions voluntarily? If she can't, is someone available to regularly take her to the bathroom or assist her if she soils herself? Is there a comfortable room for Mom to sleep in? Will she have anyone to assist her in participating in meaningful activities? What will her daily schedule be like? Will her anticipated schedule work into the family schedule? If not, what adjustments need to be made? If Mom has memory impairment, does she exhibit any behaviors that may be disruptive to the family? If so, what are these behaviors and how will they be handled? (See Chapter 15.) Do you anticipate any dangers to the health and safety of Mom or the family, if she stays in your home?

These are just some of the questions that should be discussed by all of the family members. I suggest that you develop a plan of care or assistance for your parent, prior to having her come live with you. This plan should be updated and changed as the need arises.

This chapter is not meant to discourage adult children from bringing elderly parents home to live with them. Having an elderly parent live with you may be a rewarding, loving, mutually beneficial experience. Just plan ahead and prepare for potential challenges along the way. Also have an alternative plan in case you try bringing a parent home and it doesn't work out. Don't wait until your parent is in severe need or you and your family are burned out before you make alternative arrangements. (See Chapters 8-12, on alternative living arrangements.) Keep both your parent, yourself and your entire family in mind at all times.

If you decide to have Mom or Dad live with you in your home, or if you plan to help them remain independently in their own home, the rest of this chapter will be valuable. Home can be the best place for an elderly person, especially if services can be brought in to assist in maximizing or maintaining independent function and quality of life. Let's begin by developing a plan of care and learning how to address some of the questions asked earlier in this chapter.

To be successful in managing an elderly person in the home, one needs to be able to accurately assess needs and match those needs with available services. As a caregiver, in order to find out what the needs of your elderly parent may be, you must gather information. You can develop what I call a challenge list. On one side of a piece of paper, write down all of the challenges that face your elderly parent, such as grocery shopping, paying bills, staying alone during the day, taking medications, getting to and from doctor appointments, showering twice per week. I suggest that you complete the challenge inventory below, making any additions you can think of and reviewing the results with your family and doctor.

Listed below are some common caregiving tasks. If you assist your elderly loved one with any of the following tasks, indicate how much assistance you give and how much of a burden you perceive the task to be for you.

In the first space at left, indicate the level of assistance necessary; let 1 = none, 2 = minimal, 3 = moderate, 4 = extensive.

In the second space at left, indicate your perception of level of burden; let **1** = none, **2** = minimal, **3** = moderate, **4** = extensive.

_____ _____ 1. shopping
_____ _____ 2. paying bills/managing finances
_____ _____ 3. arranging appointments
_____ _____ 4. driving to and from appointments
_____ _____ 5. house cleaning
_____ _____ 6. administration or monitoring of medications
_____ _____ 7. providing for activity or recreation
_____ _____ 8. arranging help in the home
_____ _____ 9. arranging and attending doctor visits
_____ _____ 10. visiting regularly
_____ _____ 11. providing reassurance and companionship
_____ _____ 12. responding to emergencies
_____ _____ 13. dressing
_____ _____ 14. bathing
_____ _____ 15. meal preparation
_____ _____ 16. eating
_____ _____ 17. walking
_____ _____ 18. transferring from one position to another
_____ _____ 19. grooming and personal hygiene
_____ _____ 20. going to the bathroom
_____ _____ 21. dealing with difficult behaviors

Ask the doctor to refer you to a home health agency, social worker or nurse who will come to your home to assist you in developing your plan of care. You may also look in the phone book or check with local senior centers to find out what organizations in your area will assist in home care evaluations. Many areas even have information and referral lines specifically set up to offer assistance finding necessary help. Look in your local phone book under government services for the Area Agency on Aging or check with your state department on aging, listed in the back of this book, for information available in your local area. Perhaps you can get information from them on available services to help in the home. Your local hospital's social services department is also a good resource when you need information on how to get someone to come to the home to do an evaluation.

If you enlist the help of professionals, participate as much as possible in the home evaluation process. Any information you can provide is valuable, and your involvement will be a learning process. When developing a challenge list, keep in mind that, over time, challenges come and go. New challenges develop and old challenges may get worse or subside.

At times, some caregivers tend to do too much for a parent or spouse; they don't let the person for whom they are caring be an active participant in the plan of care. Allow participation, autonomy and as much independence as possible, when assisting your loved one with home care. If she is informed and consulted, chances are that she will participate and cooperate with the arrangements being made.

When you believe that an accurate, realistic challenge list has been created, it is time to make some goals and plans to help you meet the home care challenges. You may need to prioritize if the necessary resources to meet the challenges are not available. If resources must be rationed, health and safety needs probably should have the highest priority. Below are some common challenges, goals and plans for care with which I have assisted people. You can adapt these to meet the specific needs that you and your elderly loved one have.

Challenge: *Mom is afraid to be alone.*

Goal: *Will discuss Mom's fears with her in detail and ask what she is afraid of. Is she really afraid, or is she just lonely? I will ask Mom what she thinks can be done to help her to be more comfortable when she is alone.*

Notes: *After Mom and I discussed her fears, I realized that she is afraid of falling and not being able to reach anyone for help. She also feels lonely and isolated, and the fear that she expresses is her way of reaching out for the children to come and visit more often.*

Plans: *To ease Mom's fear of falling, we will evaluate the house for safety. [See Chapter 4.] Phones will be put in each room—including the bathroom—so that Mom can telephone for help if she needs it. An emergency alert response system will be investigated. The children will develop a visit and call schedule, which will maximize the number of calls and visits that can be made. We will work together with Mom to assist her in making some close friends in the neighborhood. We will check at the local senior center to see what activities are available. Over the next thirty days we will talk with Mom about her fear of being alone and see how she is coping.*

Challenge: *Mom isn't eating properly.*
Goal: *Determine how Mom should be eating and what is keeping her from eating properly. Is she depressed? Does she have a poor appetite? Difficulty with chewing? Is she unable to prepare meals? If she used to be able to prepare meals, what is stopping her from doing so now? Is there anything that could be done to adapt the kitchen or kitchen equipment to assist her in cooking again?*

When developing a home care plan, you need to ask plenty of questions. If Mom's cooking ability is limited only because she cannot open cans or cut vegetables with existing utensils, adaptive equipment may be needed. A referral to an occupational therapist would be helpful in this case. The occupational therapist will come to the home and help adapt the kitchen and utensils to meet the ability or disability of the user. A home nursing agency or physician can refer you to an occupational therapist. If Mom's arthritis keeps her from reaching pots and pans or turning the stove on and off, adaptations can be made to enable her to negotiate the cooking process. "Meals on Wheels" may be available in your area; you should check with your local senior center or hospital discharge planner to see if your parent is eligible. "Meals on Wheels" is a home delivery meal program for people who can no longer manage meal preparation. Be creative by asking neighbors to help. Perhaps a family nearby will assist in shopping and meal preparation for a nominal fee. Maybe a responsible teenager who lives in Mom's neighborhood would help to prepare meals after school.

If grocery shopping is a problem and you're unable as a caregiver to devote the time to shopping, check to see if there is a local grocery store that will deliver. If not, again, perhaps you can make use of a neighbor or responsible teenager in the neighborhood. If Mom's shopping and meal preparation needs are met but she is still not eating, then you need to look for other problems. Poor appetite and weight loss can be a sign of depression or illness. Bring this to the attention of your loved one's doctor, and get a thorough evaluation.

> **Challenge:** *Mom needs transportation to and from doctor appointments, and I don't have time to take her.*
> **Goal:** *Arrange for Mom to receive necessary services when she needs them.*

Check your local area's senior centers or transportation companies; find out if there is a dial-a-ride program available to pick up seniors to take them to appointments. If so, see how much it costs and if it is appropriate for your parent.

The limitation to such a program is that often it only picks up and drops off the elderly people at their destinations. If your parent is too frail to get from the parking lot into the doctor's office without help, you may need to hire someone to take her and stay with her. Check with her neighbors or hire a part-time helper whose duties include driving. Make sure the person has a good car and insurance before you do the hiring. In coordinating home care, I follow the axiom that if you can't bring the person to the service, you should bring the service to the person. If transportation to the doctor is difficult, spend your time trying to find a doctor who makes house calls. There are such doctors, and they may actually begin to increase in number, as the population is aging and the elderly require easier access to care. A house call also allows the doctor to get a complete picture of how your parent is functioning—information that he or she wouldn't normally get in the office. Your parent may also feel more comfortable and powerful if the doctor visits in the home.

If you are concerned about whether your parent should still drive, you should read Chapter 6, "When Driving Becomes Unsafe."

Take a moment now to write a list of challenges that your elderly parent is currently facing or may be facing in the near future. After the list is complete, make another list of the strengths your elderly parent has and of ways you can assist her in meeting her challenges. Share this list with your parent, and have her add to or take away from it. This exercise may assist in developing the home care program and preventing premature or unnecessary institutionalization.

The most difficult challenge to manage in the home is providing nursing or personal assistance with activities such as dressing, bathing, walking, and getting to the bathroom. In gerontology we call these basic functions "activities of daily living." If your parent is dependent in one or more of these areas, maintaining her at home may require assistance of a nurse's aide or companion. If her care needs are medically complex, you may find it necessary to bring a licensed nurse into the home.

Bringing help into the home is difficult. Good people are hard to find and even harder to keep. Once a helper is hired, it is difficult to monitor the care your parent is receiving unless you check daily. You should have a backup plan available, so that if the aide doesn't show up one day, necessary help will still be provided to your parent. What are your options? By this time you are an expert on the needs of your elderly loved one. Once you know what your parent's needs are, you can match her needs with a potential helper's available time and level of experience.

In order to find help, you must know where to look. You can find home health agencies and nurses registries in the phone book, or you can get referrals from your doctor or hospital discharge planning department. Bringing help into the home will cost money. The amount will depend upon how many hours of help are required per day, the qualifications of the help needed, and the eligibility of your loved one to receive home health services under Medicare or a private insurance program. You should check on available home health services in the specific area where your parent lives and find out how much is covered by government subsidized programs. Usually, if you cannot get the information from the doctor or hospital discharge planner, the local Social Security office or Area Agency on Aging will help in your search.

Home health services, in order to be covered by Medicare, must be provided by a Certified Home Health Agency. For an agency to be certified to participate in the Medicare program, it must meet certain criteria. These agencies usually provide help in the home after an elderly person is discharged from the hospital following an acute illness. Coverage of such services may be limited to a specified number of days and hours (per day). Unless the homebound, elderly patient has a condition that requires intermittent skilled nursing or therapy, she may not be covered by Medicare. The home services provided by a Medicare certified home health agency must be ordered by your parent's physician. You may ask the doctor to order home care. Chances are, the doctor will order it; then a home care nurse or social worker from the agency will come to do an intake evaluation. The nurse or social worker can answer your questions and let you know how much, if any, care will be provided and covered under the Medicare program.

Another option is a nurses registry, which simply hires staff and coordinates visits to the elderly person's home. The agency may pay the helper $6.00 per hour and bill you $10.00 per hour for the services. Using an agency is supposed to provide you with peace of mind to know that you will be getting a reliable helper with good references. This doesn't always happen, however, so give careful consideration to choosing the agency, and monitor the person whom they are sending to assist your parent. Most agencies are competent and try to provide good people. Remember, however, that their incentive is to provide as many hours as they can. If they can hire less qualified people at lower pay rates, they can also make more money when they charge you their standard fee. If you do decide to use a nurses agency, try to use one that will send out a professional nurse or social worker to evaluate the needs of your parent. Ask to meet and approve any helpers they may be sending, and allow your parent to meet and choose somebody she likes.

You may wish to consider alternatives to certified home health agencies and nurses registries. You can try to hire a caregiver on your own. You can place an ad in the newspaper, advertising the type of person you want, along with hours and pay. Be sure to interview the potential caregiver at your home, first. If the person responding is not trustworthy or preys on the elderly, disclosing your parent's phone number and address can be dangerous. It simply gives the criminal an address and phone number for a potentially helpless victim.

Check with local nursing schools to see if they will post an ad on their bulletin board or in their job bank. Often, students would love the opportunity to work with an elderly person and earn extra spending money. If an extra bedroom is available, you may wish to consider a live-in helper who would offer care in exchange for room and board and a slight fee. You need to tailor your plan of care around the amount of home help needed and the financial resources available.

If you do choose somebody who, you feel, will be offering help in the home on a regular basis, put your agreement in writing, so that there is no question about what everyone's responsibility is. Check references prior to hiring, and if possible, check for criminal records with the local police department. If you can arrange it, meet at least weekly with the hired helper and your parent to see how things are going. Don't wait until it is too late to resolve any problems that are developing.

Describing how to actually do hands-on care of the elderly,

such as bathing assistance, dressing, and toilet transferring is beyond the scope of this book.

Whether you are doing the hands-on care yourself or you hire someone to do it, be aware of the basics. Supplement what you learn in this book by reading a book on basic home care nursing. Such books are available in the library or bookstore and cover specifics on things such as giving a bed bath; lifting a dependent person without getting injured; assisting a dependent person in dressing, bathing, toileting and grooming; helping a person to walk; performing range-of-motion exercises to maintain joint mobility. In addition, these books cover other topics specifically related to nursing care.

Other chapters in this book offer valuable information on providing care for your parent, whether she is at home or in an institution. Try to apply this information to your specific, unique set of caregiving circumstances.

As Dorothy said when she clicked the heels of her ruby slippers in the Land Of Oz, "There's no place like home. There's no place like home. There's no place like home."

Those five words seem fitting when caring for an elderly loved one. Home can be a great place for an elderly parent if her needs are being met properly. Home can be an awful place for an elderly parent if she is isolated, feels unsafe, and is not receiving the assistance she needs. You face an awesome responsibility when you assist a parent in managing care at home. Sometimes you will want to throw in the towel and move a parent to a nursing home or retirement facility. These issues are discussed in subsequent chapters at great length. Just remember that things will never go perfectly, especially when you are dealing with people. Don't expect perfection from your parent, yourself, or the people you bring into the home to help. Bringing help into the home may improve the quality of your parent's life, make things worse, or have no effect at all. Just be proud and happy that you're doing the best you can to help a loved one in need.

ADULT DAY CARE CENTERS

Before ending this chapter on home care, the reader should know about the support services offered by Adult Day Care Centers. Adult day care centers are important options for caregivers and their elderly family members who are at risk for premature institutionalization. Adult day care centers provide daytime supervision and services to the elderly which may include intermittent nursing care; physical, occupational and speech therapy; meals; therapeutic recreation; and support for caregivers. Often, transportation is provided to and from day care centers for families who are not able to provide transportation on their own.

The main benefit of adult day care centers is that caregivers can get necessary relief while their elderly family member is at the day care center. Because an elderly loved one is receiving care and supervision during the day, the caregiver can go to work and not have to quit her job in order to stay at home and provide care. Costs of these services may vary from area to area, and are sometimes subsidized by Medicaid or insurance. Even if the cost is not subsidized, adult day care may be less expensive than nursing homes or hiring private help to assist an elderly loved one during the day. The social and emotional benefits to the elderly participant in adult day care may also be of great value. Adult day care centers are different from senior centers in that they provide care and supervision for a *dependent* elderly person. Certain criteria may have to be met in order for your elderly family member to qualify because some day care centers are not set up to handle problems such as incontinence, total dependence in walking or transferring, or problem behaviors. I would suggest you investigate the adult day care option in a similar fashion as I outlined in chapters on how to choose a nursing home or retirement center. Referrals to adult day care centers may be obtained from your local hospital discharge planner or Area Agency on Aging. These numbers can be found in the phone book or by calling directory assistance. The National Institute On Adult Day Care/National Council On The Aging, 600 Maryland Avenue, S.W., W. Wing 100, Washington, D.C. 20024, 202-479-6680, may also offer information and lists of adult day care centers in your area.

8

ALTERNATIVE LIVING ARRANGEMENTS

RETIREMENT CENTERS

THERE ARE MANY TYPES OF ALTERNATIVE living arrangements available to the elderly. Most facilities offer a wide variety of services at different prices. Retirement facilities, at the very least, offer a place to live, with meals and minimal housekeeping services. When your loved one can no longer live at home independently, a retirement facility may be an appropriate alternative to living at home.

"Honey, I'm worried about Mom."

"You're always worried about your mom, and she's starting to require a lot of your time and attention. As a matter of fact, your mom is starting to cause tension in our marriage, and we have to do something about it."

"What kind of son-in-law are you? You're being very insensitive. If it were your mom, you wouldn't be talking this way, and I would be supportive of you."

"Well, I still think something has to be done. You're her daughter, and I think you're being too emotional about the whole situation. Why don't we move your mom to one of those retirement places or something?"

"She's my mom, and I have a right to be emotional. When I was acting up as a teenager, she didn't move me to a reform school 'or something.' Besides, before Dad died I promised him that I'd be sure that Mom would be taken care of."

"Well why doesn't your brother call or help once in a while? He has some responsibility as a son, doesn't he?"

"You know he and Mom haven't gotten along since he married out of the faith. Do you think they're going to start getting along now?"

"I don't know, but why should we have all of the responsibility?"

"I can't believe you're talking this way about my mom—the grandmother to our children!"

"Be realistic, sweetheart. The neighborhood your mom lives in isn't safe anymore. I feel uneasy when you and the kids go visit her. She can't make meals or go shopping anymore, so you spend at least one day every week over there, making sure she's fed. She goes to the doctor so much that you seem to be driving her around more than you drive the kids. She's called at least three times in the past month—after midnight—because she was afraid someone was breaking into the house or because she couldn't get up off the bed. She does nothing all day but sit in her little house and watch television. She can't do any of the cleaning, and she doesn't even enjoy her garden anymore, because she can't bend over to tend the flowers. I'm just her son-in-law. I'm not a doctor, but I think it's time to help her move to some kind of retirement place before it's too late."

"I guess you're right, but I wish you'd be kinder and more understanding when we discuss my mother. I'll start looking for places first thing in the morning. I know I'm going to have quite a time getting Mom to leave that house, though. She has more than thirty years of memories tied up in it. Honey, I'm going to need your support through this. O.K.?"

"O.K., dear, that's what husbands and sons-in-law are for."

There may come a time when your parent can no longer stay alone at home and home care options have been exhausted or aren't feasible. When this time comes, you may need to learn about retirement options. The next few chapters will focus on retirement hotels, continuing care retirement centers, board and care homes, and assisted living centers. Also, a complete chapter in this book focuses on nursing home care and placement. The scenario played out between the husband and wife above is very common and quite distressing. Knowing your options will help alleviate some of the stress and make painful decisions more comfortable for all.

The first step in choosing which facility is best for your loved one is to come to a clear understanding of the needs of your loved one. When choosing a retirement facility, your choice may depend upon how much assistance is offered and at what point your loved one will be required to move to a nursing or assisted living center. There are so many types of boarding arrangements or retirement facilities for the elderly that it is difficult to determine what type is best. Different states have diverse regulations on the amount of care that a center must offer in order to qualify for various licensing categories. Therefore, as a potential consumer, you must be aware and ask a lot of questions. In approaching the issue of finding the appropriate type of facility for your loved one, you will want to make judgments at two levels. First, evaluate your loved one's care needs. Second, assess each potential facility's ability to provide care in at least the following areas: walking, bathing, medication administration, toileting, dressing, eating, medical supervision, transportation, social and recreational programming, and housekeeping and laundry services. Ask questions and get specific answers before you choose a facility. This is absolutely necessary. If you don't make a thorough evaluation before you choose, you may find yourself spending just as much time caring for your loved one in the retirement facility as you did in your own or your loved one's home. Ambulation, or walking requirements, of your loved one is crucial. Ask the potential facility personnel if walkers and wheelchairs are allowed and to what extent they may be used. If your loved one needs a walker and/or wheelchair, be sure that the facility has a physical plant to accommodate an assistive device and has the proper fire clearance from the local fire authority. If your loved one will be moving into a fifth floor retirement apartment and needs a walker to walk, chances are that she would not be able to get down five flights of stairs in a fire, by herself. Inquire whether walkers and wheelchairs are allowed, and ask what will happen if your loved one who previously walked independently has to temporarily or permanently use a walker or wheelchair. If the facility will make your loved one move out, and you believe she will be needing a walker soon, it would be wise to choose a retirement facility licensed and able to accept residents who do not walk independently. An alternative may be to choose a first floor accommodation and a room closer to the dining area. If your loved one needs assistance with bathing or will soon need such assistance, inquire as to what, if any, assistance the facility offers. Are rooms equipped with grab bars in the shower? Is the bathing area adapted to fit the needs of an elderly disabled person? How often are baths given and by whom? Does the resident get to choose bath times, or are they assigned? If residents do not ask for a bath, are they encouraged to maintain personal hygiene?

Are staff people trained to assist the elderly with bathing? Are such things as resident safety and regulation of the water temperature monitored? Are there emergency call cords in the bathroom, in case your loved one falls and is unable to call for help?

If your loved one needs assistance with taking medications properly, inquire as to whether this type of help is available in a potential retirement facility. Find out who will administer the medication to your loved one, and ask about the type of training he or she has. At a minimum, you should feel comfortable that the one giving the medication will be able to properly identify the person to whom the medication is being given, will give the proper medicine at the proper dosage, will have an idea what the medicine is used for (as well as signs and symptoms of adverse reactions), and will be in contact with your loved one's physician if medicines need to be initiated or discontinued. Does the facility have a centralized place to store medications, and are the medications administered at the prescribed times? Does the facility have a contract with a pharmacy that delivers medications, or do you have to bring medication in for your loved one when the doctor orders it? Are you required to use the facility pharmacy, and if so, does it have reasonable prices? If your loved one should need injections, does the facility have the ability to safely administer injectable medications?

If your loved one becomes incontinent, does the facility offer incontinent care, or will she be asked to move out? If the facility does accept incontinent residents, how is the incontinence managed? At a minimum, residents should be kept clean and dry and should be encouraged and helped to use the bathroom on a regular schedule. If incontinent briefs and pads are used, they should be checked and changed as necessary. The loss of control of urine or feces can be devastating to an elderly person, and care should be offered in the most dignified, comfortable way possible. Be frank, and ask exactly how much incontinence care is offered and how much such extra care will cost.

If your loved one needs assistance in dressing, is such assistance offered, and are residents encouraged to learn how to dress independently? Do they get to choose what they will wear and when they should get dressed and undressed?

If your loved one no longer can cook or make meals independently, it would be wise to choose a retirement home that offers three balanced meals per day. On your tour of the facility, ask for a sample menu and observe the food preparation and service. Facilities that offer choices of meals and select menus may be an encouragement for your loved one to eat properly. Ask if all meals must be eaten in the dining room or if the facility offers room service for those not wanting to be in a group setting. Inquire about the times of meals and ask if between-meal snacks are available. If your loved one is on a diabetic, a low salt, or another therapeutic diet, check to see if the retirement facility has the ability to prepare and offer such meals. Also inquire if the meals are supervised by a licensed dietitian.

If your loved one has difficulty walking or tires easily, be sure to choose an apartment or room close to the dining area, so that the distance doesn't discourage going to meals. Inquire about seating arrangements in the dining area. Do people get to choose where they sit, or is there assigned seating? Meals may be a major event of the day for many elderly people, and you may witness this in retirement facilities as people line up to be seated in the dining room. Many people may go an hour early, just to fill time or get the seat they want. Observe how the staff interacts with the people waiting for meals. Are they friendly and courteous? Are there any social or activity programs going on in the waiting area to keep residents alert and occupied? Are meals served on time? Are they warm and attractively prepared? Are the portions adequate, and are residents allowed to take leftovers back to their rooms for snacks later in the day? Do servers talk with the residents and offer substitutes for items one may not like? Is there someone in charge of the dining room at each meal, in case a resident chokes or needs attention?

If there is a select menu, is assistance provided for residents who need help in filling out the menu? Are the residents who eat slowly rushed out of the dining room, or are they allowed to stay until finished? Are chairs and tables at a comfortable, safe, height for residents? Ask these questions about meal service in the retirement facility which you are investigating, and observe a few meals. Some facilities may even invite you to eat with your loved one to try the food. As with many other service industries, the price you pay for the service may dictate the quality. If you know what questions to ask and what to observe, you can still compare apples with apples and oranges with oranges. Perhaps the food in one facility is better than in another similarly priced facility, but the physical plant is a bit older and not as pretty. It is up to you and your loved one to make an informed choice about what is more important.

What type of supervision and staffing are available in the retirement facility? Ask how many people are on duty during the day and night and what level of training they have. Is there a nurse available to assess a change of medical condition and report the change to the physician? Is basic first aid offered? Are there emergency call cords in residents' rooms? If so, who responds to the emergency and how long does it take? Does the facility have a resident assurance system to check on residents who do not come down for meals or who have not left their rooms? This question is very important for the family and resident's peace of mind; in a large retirement facility with no assurance system, a resident could lie, helpless, for days before being discovered and helped. Does the facility have a physician, podiatrist, optometrist and other health professionals available to make house calls? If not, does the facility offer transportation to and from appointments? If the facility offers transportation, how far in advance do appointments have to be made? Is the bus safe, in good repair and able to transport the handicapped comfortably? Is the driver licensed and able to safely drive the retirement facility vehicle? Is there an extra charge for transportation? Does the facility maintain liability insurance for the facility vehicle?

How far away from the facility will the transportation services drive? This is an important question. If your loved one's doctor is ten miles away from the retirement home and the retirement home transportation will only drive a five-mile radius around the facility, you want to know it before choosing it as a residence.

Does the transportation service merely drop your loved one off at the front of a building, or will they have a staff member assist her into a doctor's office, wait through the appointment, and help return her safely to the transportation vehicle at the scheduled time? Ask all of these questions, and be sure to get complete answers. All of the facilities you visit may say they offer transportation, but when you truly investigate, some facilities' transportation services may be far superior to others.

When choosing a retirement facility for your loved one, try to choose one that has a social service or resident service director available to assist with psycho-social needs. If your loved one is lonely, depressed, or merely in need of assistance in arranging appointments, social services personnel can offer a tremendous amount of assistance. Just having a resident advocate, someone on the staff to whom a resident can talk, will make a difference in the spirit of a facility. Ask if there is a resident council in the facility and whether residents have any input into how the facility is operated. Most good facilities take into account the wants and desires of residents; they are encouraged to offer input into the daily operation of the retirement center.

Inquire about what type of recreational activities the facility offers, and get a copy of the recreation schedule. Are the programs diverse and of interest to your loved one? Is there entertainment offered? Are there outings away from the facility? Are religious services offered regularly? Does the facility have a staff member in charge of recreation, and does this person give the residents a choice of what programs should be offered?

Does the facility have a gift and beauty shop? If so, what items and services are available and what is the cost? If your loved one is not able to do cleaning or laundry, are these services offered in the retirement facility? If so, is there an additional charge? How often are rooms cleaned and linen replaced? Is personal laundry included in the linen service? Is housekeeping done on a regular schedule? If so, does the resident get to choose when her room will be cleaned? Are you responsible for the maintenance of the room if something breaks or spills on the floor? Does the facility have a maintenance staff member to fix what breaks in a timely manner? When your loved one moves, are you responsible for painting or patching the room at your expense?

If you look in the senior newspaper, you can find dozens of advertisements for retirement communities. Each of them advertises what seems to be the same amenities: active living, gourmet meals, caring staff, housekeeping, laundry and security, and well appointed, spacious accommodations. As consumers, it's difficult to choose between them. I recommend that you bring your loved one with you to each community you visit and let her be actively involved in the decision. Some places just have a good spirit about them, even if the building and surroundings are not very fancy. Ask to meet the administrator of the facility and get a feeling from him or her about the operation of the facility and the owner(s)'s philosophy. In most businesses—especially those which care for the elderly—attitudes and management style filter from the top of the organization, down. If the administrator is educated in aging and caring and knows the residents and staff, there is a good chance that he/she runs a good, honest, caring, solid operation. Ask the administrator to show you around. If he knows the residents by name and you witness interaction with residents during the tour, then chances are that he is responsive to the residents' needs.

Ask about any special rules and regulations that apply to residents at the retirement center. Some retirement centers have a resident handbook that you can review. Can you bring furniture and pets? Can you hang pictures, change drapes or alter the apartment in any way? Can children visit and stay overnight in the resident's apartment? If so, for how long? How much notice must be given before moving out? Are refunds given for days the resident does not occupy the apartment? Read the admission agreement carefully, and ask questions about anything that isn't clear to you. When comparing different retirement communities, you should check prices. What is the monthly charge and what, exactly, does it cover? Get a list of additional charges for such things as beauty shop, transportation, meal delivery, incontinent care, showering, nursing assistance, and laundry. Ask how often the rent is raised and by how much. If the facility has been in operation for a year or more, ask for figures on the date and amount of the last three rent increases.

Make a few visits to the retirement center at different times of the day and on weekends. Observe the staff and resident activities and supervision. Ask if it's possible for your loved one to stay in a guest apartment for a week to see if she likes the facility. The elderly are a very heterogeneous group, and different retirement communities have a wide variety of occupants. Look around to see if the age and physical ability level of the residents is matched closely to your elderly parent. If your mother is dynamic, social, and still mobile for her age, she may not be happy interacting with women who are older and less capable. Location may be of prime importance to both the elderly parent and the adult child. Location of communities also has a direct impact on cost. Retirement communities in wealthier areas may be more expensive. Retirement communities located in areas where many elderly live may have lower costs due to the immense concentration of facilities and the number of empty, available apartments. You have to decide whether monthly cost is more important than proximity to family, doctors, and previous community friends. Just be aware that costs for almost identical services can differ tremendously between cities and towns.

When discussing and planning for cost of a retirement community, be sure to ask if the facility participates in any public assistance programs, in case your parent's assets run out during her stay at the facility. If both of your parents are moving to the retirement facility, what is the policy if one of them dies? Does the monthly fee decrease? If your father is receiving a pension that does not revert to your mother upon death, what happens if your mother can no longer afford the monthly payment at the retirement center? Can she get a roommate to supplement her monthly payment? Finally, if you have the time, ask the residents of the retirement community how they like it. The residents may be your best source of information.

9

LIFE CARE

CONTINUING CARE
RETIREMENT COMMUNITIES
FOR THE ELDERLY

CONTINUING CARE RETIREMENT COMMUNITIES (CCRCs), often called life care communities, offer a wide variety of living arrangements and services to the elderly. These types of communities differ from rental retirement centers in several key areas. When moving to a CCRC, the resident pays an entrance fee that can range from thirty- to three-hundred thousand dollars. In exchange for the initial entrance fee, the resident signs a life care contract that usually guarantees the resident care for life in the community. Should a resident become ill and more dependent, services may be offered for free or at a reduced cost at the CCRC health center. In most cases the resident is guaranteed care, even if her financial resources are exhausted. The term "life care" implies care for the rest of one's life. It is this promise that makes these types of retirement communities so attractive to a growing number of elderly people.

Choosing to move to a CCRC is a big decision, because of the large up-front investment that is required to enter the community. Most elderly people sell the home in which they've lived for several years and use the equity to pay the entrance fee at the CCRC.

There are several advantages to the type of living arrangements a CCRC offers. Many elderly people do not wish to be a burden to their children and are concerned about the potential long term financial burden of nursing home care, in case a disabling illness occurs. CCRCs help to alleviate these concerns because of the health care guarantee given in the contract. CCRCs are set up with continuity of care and service in mind. The campus, as it is called, usually has independent living, assisted care, and skilled nursing available. Because all levels of care are offered in the same community, spouses do not have to become separated should one become ill. In addition, the staff and residents of the community feel a sense of fellowship; residents are never among strangers, should long term care be needed. To occupy an independent living apartment, one must pay a monthly service fee, as would be the case in a rental retirement community. These monthly service fees, however, are generally much lower than rental community fees, because of the initial investment required to enter a CCRC. CCRCs offer a variety of independent living apartments with amenities such as meal service, housekeeping, laundry, transportation, security, nursing, recreation, social service, assurance and emergency response, and an on-site health center.

Choosing an appropriate CCRC is much more difficult than choosing a rental retirement community, because you are shopping for much more. In addition to choosing a nice place to live, you must understand the contract for care that is being offered. You must also determine whether your initial entrance fee is protected. CCRCs work much like insurance companies, in the sense that they spread the risk of illness or asset depletion over the group of residents who move in. If they admit people who are very ill into an independent living apartment, those residents may consume free care at a faster than normal rate. If too many people are admitted who are not financially qualified, the community may be burdened by people who cannot pay their bills.

It is very important to investigate the financial integrity of any CCRC in which your elderly parents are considering investing. There have been a number of these types of communities that, after taking the entrance fees of elderly residents, have subsequently gone bankrupt. If you invest in a poorly managed or undercapitalized community, you can lose your life savings. Even if the CCRC is a non-profit religious organization, you should do a thorough investigation before allowing your parents to move in.

State regulation of CCRCs varies from state to state, and you should check with the licensing board in the state in which the CCRC is located to see if the operation complies with state requirements. CCRC personnel should be able to tell you whom to call. Ask to review financial statements of the community to see if it is operating in the black and has money reserved for the future.

The average person cannot interpret financial reports. You may wish to have your accountant review the information and ask the CCRC representative necessary questions in order to determine the financial integrity of the operation. If possible, try to choose a community that has paid off its mortgage and construction loans with the initial entrance fees of residents. If there is no third party debt on the community, there is less chance that a bank can foreclose if the community gets into financial trouble. Investigate the owners and other communities they operate, to see if they are in any financial trouble. Here, again, is a point at which it is important to get the advice of an accountant experienced in this area, as well as a good attorney who is experienced in estate planning, before choosing a community.

Different CCRCs offer diverse entrance fee refunds and health care guarantees. Some CCRCs keep a portion of the entrance fee and refund a certain percentage based upon the amount of time the resident lived in the community. For example, the resident may pay an entrance fee of $100,000 and be guaranteed a refund of at least 50% or $50,000 upon death or termination of the contract. The other 50% may go to the CCRC over a specified time period. In some CCRCs, one pays an entrance fee and gets no refund at all. You may pay and lose the entrance fee at 5% the first year, 20% the second year, and 25% each year for the next three years until the entrance fee is gone. Usually the communities that offer smaller entrance fee refunds also give more free health care. Try to choose a community that offers at least some of the entrance fee back. Also be sure that the entrance fee is held in some sort of trust or escrow so that the money is available should your parent leave the community or die. Health care is usually offered at a reduced rate to CCRC residents, or a specified or unlimited amount of free care is offered. Find out just how much care is offered and at what cost. For example: If both of your parents move in and the contract guarantees 500 free days of care at the health center, is that 500 free days for each of your parents or is the total number of free health care days available per apartment split as 250 days for each parent? Who determines whether the health care is necessary—the resident's personal physician or the CCRC staff? How do the costs change if one parent is living permanently in the health center and one remains in the independent living apartment? How long can a resident keep the independent living apartment if she is ill in the health center? What happens if the health center is full and doesn't have room to accept your parent should the need arise?

What type of care is provided in the health center and are there any health conditions that cannot be handled? If your parents should run out of funds, what is the procedure for their continued care? Do they have to prove that they didn't give money away to children? If they lose their money in a bad investment and can no longer afford to pay for their care, will the CCRC supplement them financially? Can your parents borrow against the refundable portion of their entrance fee should the need arise?

The continuing care retirement community can be a very wise investment, and life in such a community can be pleasant and secure. These types of life care arrangements will probably be the wave of the future for those who can qualify physically or financially for entrance. As with everything else discussed in this book, it is important to do a thorough investigation and ask a lot of questions before entry. As a final note, I caution you to get the advice of an accountant about how the IRS views the money given to CCRCs as entrance fees. There may be some tax consequences when your parents pay capital gains from the sale of their home and pay imputed interest on the entrance fee. Have your accountant and lawyer thoroughly review the life care contract before you make the investment. For many elderly, this is a wise investment in the future, if the community being considered is properly managed and financially sound.

10

SMALL BOARD AND CARE HOMES

A SMALL, PRIVATE, BOARD AND CARE HOME may be a good living arrangement for an elderly parent who needs assistance but doesn't want to live in an institutional environment. Small homes are usually licensed by the Department of Social Services and generally house between two to six residents. Many of these homes are operated by private parties who actually live in and offer care to the elderly clients in a single family dwelling.

Regulation of these small homes is very difficult due to their numbers, wide geographical distribution, and lack of regulators to inspect and monitor care. Because of the possibility of regulators not being able to supervise the quality of care in these homes, it is important that you choose a good home and keep an eye on how your parent is being treated.

Many of these private boarding homes are just like homes you and I occupy. The positive aspect of this living arrangement is obvious. Your parent will live in an environment that resembles home and will not have to deal with institutional living. Negative aspects of this living arrangement may not be so obvious, so you need to be on the alert. Private boarding homes may be understaffed or may have staff who aren't trained in caring for the elderly. The home may not be physically adapted to meet the needs of an elderly person. Meals may be prepared that are not wholesome because of poor quality food products or ease of preparation. Activities may be absent, and your parent may end up watching television all day as she did when she was in her own home. Some private boarding homes may encourage or allow your parent to stay, even if her care needs are beyond what they can provide. The financial pressure and negative impact of losing just one resident in a small board and care home contributes to this phenomenon. A good board and care home can be a fantastic alternative when your elderly parent can no longer stay at home alone. You just need to choose the best home possible with the financial resources that are available to you.

Choosing a board and care home is similar to choosing a good retirement facility and nursing home. General approaches are found in other parts of this book. When specifically choosing a small private home to house your elderly parent, you should do a thorough investigation.

First call the local licensing agency to find out if the home in which you are interested is licensed. You can get the licensing agency's phone number from directory information or from the source that referred you to the board and care home. The phone book, doctors, social workers and friends are sources you will use to find the homes worth investigating. It may sound impolite, but I would visit the home without calling first. On your first visit, look around the neighborhood in which the home is located. Does it look safe? Is it run down? Are there parks close by for your parent to go on supervised walks? Is there a busy street that can cause a potential hazard? Walking up to the house, look to see if it is in good repair. Is the lawn mowed? Are the walkways free from hazards? Is the home gated for security? Is there a place to sit outside and visit? Are there children playing outside? Drive around the block and around the neighborhood a few times to get a feel for the surroundings.

When you go to the house, knock on the door and see how long it takes for someone to answer. If it takes several minutes for someone to come to the door or if the person answering seems bothered, perhaps staffing in the home is not adequate. Ask if you can see the home because you are interested in possibly having your parent move in. If the person does not let you in or asks you to come back later to see the home, perhaps there is a problem that is being hidden. You needn't be overly suspicious, but you should be cautious; go with your gut feeling. Ask to speak with someone in charge about your parent's care needs. If there is nobody in charge who can give you information, this in itself indicates that there may be a potential problem with supervision of care.

When you enter the home, look around. Is the interior of the home well maintained? Is it bright and cheery? Is furniture in good repair? Does the home have a smell of urine? Look at where the residents sleep. Are the beds adequate? Is linen clean and changed? Does the room smell of urine? Is there adequate space? Are there familiar things such as pictures and knick-knacks that residents at the home like? Is the room adequately lit and properly ventilated? Do sleeping quarters have an operating smoke detector? Is there an evacuation plan and a fire detection system available in the house? Is staff trained in fire safety? Are there adequate bathroom facilities? How many residents share a bathroom? Are bathrooms equipped with grab bars and non slip surfaces? Are the bathtub and shower adapted for use by the elderly? Is the hot water temperature regulated to prevent burns and scalds? Are chemicals, guns or dangerous items out of reach of the elderly clients? Is there a room for activities and relaxation, or are residents expected to stay in their bedrooms? Walk the inside and outside perimeter of the house and ask the questions above regarding the physical environment.

If you are comfortable with the physical layout of the home, you should arrange for a meeting with the owner/manager. At this meeting you should find out about the owner's experience in caring for the elderly. Does he/she have any formal training or experience in aging, nursing, or medical supervision of the elderly? I wouldn't be comfortable unless the person in charge has knowledge and credentials. Does the facility have a medical director or physician who supervises care of the residents? Is a nurse available? What are the qualifications of the staff and what are the staffing ratios? The majority of care will probably be given by nursing aides; however the aides should have at least daily or weekly supervision by a licensed nurse. What type of training does the aide have? Are the aides certified? The better the training, the safer Mom and Dad will be. Ask how many staff members are awake and on duty daily? How many of these staff members are family members who actually live in the house. If this is a small business run in the operators' family home, I would wonder if my parent were being supervised by a teenage son or daughter during part of the day or night.

You need to be assured that there is a competent adult on duty twenty-four hours a day. It is difficult to determine how many staff members are adequate for the home. Proper staffing depends upon the care needs of the residents. The home may have only four residents, but if two of these residents require a disproportionate amount of care, there may be a need for extra staff. In general, one or two people for four to six residents is adequate on a twenty-four hour basis. To feel comfortable, I would ask to meet all of the staff before bringing a parent to live at the home.

When you speak to the owner, be sure to describe the needs of your elderly parent, and ask if the home can meet her individual needs. Ask what type of care the home cannot manage and what type of care is beyond the scope of the home's license. Ask what types of activities are offered, and discuss what your parent's daily routine would be. Does the home's staff assist in medication administration? Can they provide care for incontinence? Can they assist with bathing and dressing? Can they manage problem behavior associated with memory loss and dementia? If you are aware of your parent's needs, you will find it a bit easier to determine if the facility can meet those needs. Ask about visiting hours. Visiting should be unrestricted as long as it does not interfere with care and privacy of residents. The challenge of small homes offering care to the elderly is that we tend to feel we are intruding when we visit, especially if the home is family run. If the home is operated correctly, you will feel you are part of the family, not like an intruder.

The homelike, family feeling is actually one of the advantages to this type of living arrangement. If you are comfortable with the home, the owner, and the staff, you are ready to discuss cost. What are the charges for the care that is being offered? What do the charges cover? Does the fee go up if your parent requires more care at some point in time? Do you need to sign a lease for a certain period of time? Is your money refunded if your parent dies? Is there a credit given if your parent is in the hospital or absent for an extended period of time? Be sure to get all of your financial questions answered, and try to get the charges and terms of any agreement in writing. If you think that the home is acceptable, bring your parent to visit. Perhaps she can even stay a day or two to see if the setup is satisfactory. Ask the owner for names of family members of residents currently in the home. If those family members give permission, telephone to ask how they like the home. You can also ask the home's current residents how they like living there. Because this is going to be such a confined living arrangement, it is important that the other residents in the home will get along with your parent and that your parent will fit in. Before making a final decision, check with the home's licensing board to see if there are any complaints or negative inspection reports. You can also check with the local Long Term Care Ombudsman Office to inquire about the history of the facility. Ask the home's operator for the phone numbers or for copies of any inspection reports. If things are O.K., the home's personnel will feel proud to assist you in gathering this information. Visit several homes at different times of the day, and take notes on what you liked and disliked in each home.

If operated well, small board and care homes can be a very good place to live for a frail, elderly parent no longer able to remain at home alone. Choose the home wisely, and stay involved as much as possible, to be sure the care remains adequate.

11

ASSISTED LIVING CENTERS

(PERSONAL AND INTERMEDIATE CARE)

I T HAS BEEN CLEARLY ESTABLISHED over the past several years that there are many elderly people who rest on the fence between nursing home care and care at home. These elderly people are not disabled enough to require nursing home care, yet they are not independent enough to remain in their own homes or live in a retirement hotel. To respond to the needs of these people, assisted living centers are slowly coming into fashion. Assisted living centers offer minimal to moderate assistance with medications, dressing, bathing, walking, and continence. Meals, housekeeping and activity programming are also provided.

Residents usually have their own room and can bring furniture from home. The cost of this type of care is usually somewhere between that of a retirement center and a nursing home. Residents at these facilities may range from people afraid to stay home alone to those who need intermittent nursing care.

If this type of facility is in your area, it may be a good idea to investigate the availability for your parent, if she can no longer be at home alone. To find such a facility, you can look in the yellow pages under retirement, nursing homes, rest homes or senior services. You can also call the local hospital and ask to talk to a discharge planner. Discharge planners usually know what services are available in the community.

As with the other out-of-home living facilities discussed in this book, you should do a thorough evaluation before bringing your elderly parent there to live. Ask what services are provided, by whom, and for how much. Discuss the care needs of your parent to be sure that the facility has services to match. Assisted living is a fairly new concept. It will probably gain popularity in the future, as health care costs for the elderly continue to escalate.

12

THE HOSPITAL AND
NURSING HOME EXPERIENCE

Mom had a stroke five days ago and is paralyzed on one side. She has been in the hospital since the stroke. Now, all of a sudden, they have told me that she has to leave because Medicare will not pay for her care anymore. I wish I knew what to do. It's impossible to take her home with me. She can't walk and there is no way I could lift her by myself. Even if I could lift her, I wouldn't be able to get her up the stairs to my apartment. She can't even feed herself or control her bodily functions anymore. I haven't had a chance to speak with her doctor because he only makes hospital rounds early in the morning or late at night. I have no idea what to expect. Is she going to get better, or will she be like this the rest of her life? This isn't the mother that I know. The discharge coordinator gave me a list of four nursing homes in the area to visit and says I should transfer Mom to one as soon as possible. I always promised Mom that I would not put her in a nursing home, but what choice do I have? I don't know how to begin to choose a good home, and I certainly don't know how we will afford it. Why won't someone just take the time to sit down and explain to me what I should do? Speaking of time, if I keep missing work because of hospital visits, I may lose my job. God, what a nightmare! I wish Mom would just go to sleep and be with the Lord. She wouldn't have wanted this for herself or the family. Maybe with hope and faith things will be O.K. again. I'm just so tired.

Stories like this are played out every day by families all over this country. Names, places and illnesses may be different, but the theme is the same. Families are unexpectedly thrust into an unfamiliar world of doctors, hospitals and nursing homes, not knowing where to go, how to get there, or what to do once they have arrived.

You can't always avoid or prevent a catastrophic illness, but good planning and knowing what to do in advance can make things much easier when something terrible happens. Unfortunately, the daughter in the scenario related above has no idea what to do, and to make things worse, she has very little time to make major decisions for her mother. How does this daughter really know what Mom would have wanted done if a catastrophic illness occurred? These issues should be discussed when an elderly person is well, so that everyone is comfortable with the decisions that will be made.

We plan our children's future. We choose their schools, make arrangements for someone to care for them in our absence, leave numbers of people to call in an emergency, and pray that the plans and decisions we make will be in our children's best interest. It is equally important for us to plan ahead for our parents' well-being. In order to plan ahead effectively, it is important to know what questions to ask and to whom the questions should be directed. Throughout this chapter I will try to emphasize how to get the information you need. Information is extremely valuable; in order to get the proper information, open lines of communication must be maintained at all times, regardless of feelings of anger, guilt and frustration.

In any professional caregiving situation where there are several parties involved, it is valuable to request a family meeting with the health care team. Come to the meeting prepared with a list of questions and concerns, and designate one individual as spokesperson for your family, in order to make the best use of time. If everyone attends the meeting, there is less chance of misunderstandings occurring. Families often do not agree about what should be done for their parents, and there is nothing that can make a caregiving decision more difficult than to have siblings fighting among themselves. Families are unique systems, and each child in a family may have a different agenda. One family member may remain detached and distant, while another may seem overly involved. Unfortunately, families that never were cohesive and functional don't always improve when there is a crisis with an aging parent. If an aging parent has always overcontrolled the family, this behavior may worsen when he or she is sick and fearful of losing control.

All members of the family have something to give and need to feel comfortable contributing in their way. A wealthy son may get nervous around hospitals and feel extremely uncomfortable visiting a sick parent. Perhaps this son will offer financial assistance or legal advice, or just be an open ear to a sister with no financial means but the spirit to be at the bedside. Sometimes the illness of a parent will bring a family closer because everyone is sharing a similar struggle. When looking at the solution, you must see the total picture. You are not dealing only with a parent who is in a position of need. In addition to outsiders such as doctors, nurses, social workers, and other paraprofessionals, you are also dealing with siblings and spouses of siblings who may be upset about how the illness is affecting their generation's family. For the families with whom I have worked, communication has almost universally been the key to success in coping during a parental crisis. Meet with the doctors and discharge social workers to discuss resources available to you, in light of your parent's prognosis, treatment options, and care needs. It is important for the family to request such a meeting early in the hospitalization, even if all the diagnostic information has not yet been gathered. Early meetings and discussions can help physicians direct care and possibly prevent your elderly parent from undergoing painful or unnecessary medical tests or procedures.

When in the hospital or nursing home, you may need to act as your parent's advocate when it comes time to make health care decisions. Your parent may be too ill to be able to accept informed consent, leaving you as the decision maker. It is difficult enough to make our own decisions, but to make life and death decisions for our parents is a tremendous responsibility. Advance wishes regarding intensity of care issues should be discussed with physicians and families prior to a catastrophic illness and should be put in writing. These issues are discussed in more detail in Chapter 29, "Care Near The End Of Life."

There is nothing more frustrating than being in a hospital and not having any control of one's destiny. Things tend to get done to people, and the focus is on curing an illness or gathering diagnostic information. Sometimes the human spirit is forgotten, in exchange for a lower bacterial count or a reduced tumor size. Even the best of hospitals can be dangerous for a frail, ill, elderly person. I've seen elderly patients enter the hospital with minor problems and leave bedridden and more disabled. This downward spiral experienced by a frail, hospitalized, elderly person is not caused intentionally. The problem sometimes may come from the decreased ability of the patient to adjust and recover from added stress.

Myra had remained active well into her seventies. Now at age seventy-eight, she still felt healthy when she had to enter the hospital to get an arthritic hip replaced. Because she is slightly hearing impaired, has poor memory, and can't see well, she was a bit anxious when she entered the hospital environment. The night after the surgery, she was given a post-op medicine that had an adverse effect, causing agitation and combative behavior. Because the agitation interfered with her care, a tranquilizer was prescribed. The tranquilizer caused Myra to become more confused, and she tried to get out of bed by herself. To keep Myra from falling, the nursing staff put a restraint on her. Of course, Myra didn't like to be restrained, so she slipped out of the restraint. In her tranquilized state, she climbed over the bedside rails, fell, and fractured her shoulder. With a fractured shoulder, she couldn't use a walker to start walking after the hip surgery; she had to remain immobile for the next few weeks. Because of this immobility, she developed pneumonia, which was treated with antibiotics that interfered with her appetite. At that point Myra had to be fed, because she seemed to have given up. What began as a one-week elective surgery turned into a six-week hospitalization and nine-month recovery. Myra left the hospital worse than when she went in.

What's missing in the account above? It's the intervention of a family member. I'm not suggesting that a family member always be present in the hospital to direct and coordinate care. I do believe, however, that it is important for a family member to check daily and give input in the treatment of a parent. You don't have to be a neurosurgeon to see that your parent is over-medicated or agitated. What gives family members the advantage is that they knew the elderly parent before the hospitalization, and they may recognize a change in condition sooner than the hospital staff. My advice is to be there, be aware, and don't be afraid to speak up. One last thought on hospitals revolves around tests and procedures. Medicine these days is very technologically driven, and there are a number of sub-specialists in medicine that may see your parent during a hospital stay. If the heart starts acting up, the family physician may call for a cardiology consultation. If a blood test is odd, a hematologist may be brought in. If an infection develops, an infectious disease specialist may be called. If some gastrointestinal bleeding is identified, a gastroenterologist may be summoned to do a procedure. If an x-ray or MRI is done, a radiologist will be involved. As you can see, there are a lot of doctors involved, and you may get a different story or answer from each of them. Be sure that from the get-go you find out who is the primary doctor directing care and meet with him daily. If you can't meet him face to face, write down your questions and give them to the nurse to tape to the physician progress note in the chart. If necessary, stand there and watch the nurse do this. Leave a number where you can be reached or the time you will visit next, so that the doctor can accommodate you.

Before consenting to a test or procedure for your elderly parent, you should at least ask the following questions: Is there a simpler, less invasive procedure that would furnish the same results? What are the potential side effects of the test or procedure? This is very important because frail, elderly people often have adverse reactions to medical tests that may actually worsen their conditions.

Assuming the test or procedure would yield a certain diagnosis, would it be humane or advisable to offer treatment? This is not to say that pain relief and comfort care should not be given. One must ask, however, how humane it would be to submit a frail, terminally ill 95-year-old to a bone marrow biopsy if you wouldn't treat a cancer the biopsy would diagnose.

The majority of health care professionals are honest, caring people, but you should never forget that you are your loved one's best advocate. If all else fails and you really want an honest answer to your inquiry, simply ask the physicians or nurses what they would do if it were their mother they were treating. The answer may surprise you!

THE NURSING HOME EXPERIENCE

Many times after a hospitalization, a nursing home placement is suggested on a temporary or permanent basis. Whether an elderly parent enters a nursing home from a community dwelling, board and care facility, or hospital, the major concern is usually when or if a nursing home placement is necessary. Perhaps it would be helpful to explore just what a nursing home is and what conditions are managed in nursing homes, so that the caregiver can use this information as a road map in negotiating her own situation.

Whether a nursing home placement is necessary depends upon many variables. The major variable is the amount of resources available to the elderly person's family. Many nursing home patients could be cared for at home if there were proper assistance and equipment at hand. It has been my experience that for every patient I care for in the nursing home, there is another elderly person with similar, or more extensive, disabling conditions, who is cared for at home. Whether there is placement into a nursing home may depend upon the financial and physical resources of the caregiver, rather than the condition of the elderly person in need of care.

I have not found the myth of children "dumping their parents in nursing homes" to be true. Many children and spouses do their best to provide care at home until the placement in a nursing home becomes an absolute necessity. Still others may keep a loved one at home far beyond the limits of safety and sanity.

Deciding between a loved one's moving to a nursing facility or remaining at home is often based upon emotion, not the reality of the caregiving situation. Pride, fear, guilt, anger, love, hate, cultural bias, and poor information may all be factors that contribute to the outcome of a placement decision. Having a clear picture of your loved one's care needs, as well as available resources to meet those needs, makes an emotional decision slightly more rational.

As I stated earlier, nursing home placement decisions are not just *yes* or *no*; they are also *how* and *when*. The *when to place* usually occurs if one or more of the following conditions exist without the available physical or financial resources at home to meet the needs of your elderly loved one:

- inability to control bowel and bladder functions (incontinence);
- inability to independently—or with moderate assistance—bathe, dress, walk, eat, or transfer from a lying to sitting or sitting to standing position;
- unsafe wandering or combative behavior, possibly attributed to Alzheimer's disease or a related brain disorder;
- inability to be left alone during the day or night; inability to safely manage her medications;
- multiple transfers to the acute hospital due to unmanageable medical conditions at home;
- need for rehabilitation after a stroke, fractured hip, or other acute medical crises;
- need of respite (temporary relief) for the caregiver; and
- need for nursing care and pain control near the end of life, due to a terminal illness.

To this list you can add any condition or combination of conditions that make care in the home impractical or impossible because of financial, family or physical limitations. In Chapter 7 I discuss how to care for your elderly loved one at home, and I explore various support systems that may help prevent premature or unnecessary nursing home placement.

As with most issues relating to elder care or care of one's parents, the entire family—including the parent needing nursing home care—should be involved in the decision. If possible, the family should meet and discuss the pros and cons of the move, assigning responsibilities for each member so that the transition from home to nursing facility is softened. Prepare your elderly parent for the move by being gentle and honest from the start. If you see that care at home is getting to be impossible, start discussing the possible transition a few months prior to the actual move, if possible. Of course, not every situation will leave a lot of time to prepare a loved one, especially if she is acutely ill and needing to be discharged from the hospital to the nursing home within a few days. Even in this case, however, the decision should be discussed, and the elderly parent should have some control of her destiny. Don't assume that because an elderly parent is confused or memory-impaired that she will not understand or should not be included in the decision. While a memory-impaired, frail parent may have little insight, we should offer the benefit of the doubt and explain everything that will be happening. In my experience as nursing facility administrator, I have seen adult children want to admit their elderly parents without discussing the issue or even telling them of the decision before they arrive at the door. The children are not doing this because they lack compassion. On the contrary, these adult children are so upset about the decision that they don't have the ability to openly discuss it. These are the families that usually have the biggest adjustment problems; they are the most difficult for the nursing home staff to work with. Once the decision is made, the family should be aware of what a nursing home is, how to choose a good one, how to pay for the care, and how to help the loved one and everyone else in the family adjust. These issues will be the focus of the remainder of this chapter.

What is a nursing home? The term nursing home is confusing to the lay public and conjures up emotional responses ranging from fear and disgust to peaceful pictures of a grandmother in a rocking chair, knitting a sweater. Just exactly what is this place that attracts so much public attention and elicits such emotional responses from the public? When looking for a place for your elderly parent, you may visit many different health care facilities and not exactly understand where you are or what the facility does.

Almost all facilities have to be licensed by the state in which they operate and will have the type of facility and the number of beds for which they are licensed listed on the license itself. This license should be posted in a conspicuous location in the facility for the public to view. Some facilities may be licensed for several different types of care at one location, and this information will be listed on different licenses. In general, you may hear nursing homes referred to as convalescent hospitals, nursing centers, rest homes, sanitariums, care centers, skilled nursing facilities, long term care centers, extended care centers, rehabilitation centers, or homes for the aging. If you want to find out where you are and what the facility does, just check the license in the lobby and you will get your answer.

Different facilities provide various levels of care, and it is important that you choose a facility that can meet your loved one's health, emotional and physical needs. Ask the people at the center you visit if they have the staff and equipment to care for your loved one and if the care would be within the scope of their license. When professionals refer to nursing homes, they are usually describing skilled nursing facilities. A skilled nursing facility (SNF) offers the care of licensed nurses and nursing aides on a twenty-four-hour, continuous basis. Skilled nursing facilities also offer the services of licensed therapists to carry out physicians' orders for rehabilitation. To enter an SNF, you must be admitted by a physician, and a physician must direct and monitor your care throughout the stay. If your parent needs a good deal of assistance with daily activities or rehabilitation and care after a stay in the acute hospital, you should, in most cases, be looking for placement in a skilled nursing facility. Names and levels of care may be different in various states in the United States, so be sure to check with the professionals in your area to verify your elderly parent's level of care need.

Choosing a good nursing home may be your biggest challenge. When you go looking for a home, be prepared to spend a lot of time, and be ready to ask and answer many questions. You should obtain from your loved one's physician or hospital discharge planner written information regarding the patient diagnosis, treatments, medications, self-care and nursing needs. The hospital discharge planner or physician may recommend three or more facilities to visit or may just give you a list of facilities in your local area to investigate. If you want to get some further information on the regulatory compliance of the facility on the list, you can call the Ombudsman or Department of Health Services in your area. These two agencies monitor the care in nursing homes and have public records of inspection reports and complaints. Keep in mind that a facility's having had a lot of deficiencies in certain areas doesn't necessarily mean the care is bad. You should look at the types of problems identified, as well as the severity and continued recurrence. In any case, the Health Department inspection report should be available for you to review at each nursing home you visit. If you are interested in looking at it, have a staff member go over it and explain it to you. You can get the telephone number of your local Health

Department or State Long Term Care Ombudsman Office by calling the local telephone directory information in your area.

Before choosing a facility, be sure to visit it. To get a good picture of how a facility operates, it would be wise to make at least three unscheduled visits at different times of the day. If possible, bring your elderly parent with you so that she can have input and control over her future living arrangements. If you encourage your elderly loved one to participate in the decisions, it may help in the adjustment to the nursing home placement. On your walk through the facility, make use of all of your senses. The facility will not smell of urine if the patients are given proper care. Neither should the facility smell of deodorizer or perfume, unless there is an attempt to cover urine smells. When there are a large number of elderly people who are incontinent in one building, there will be times during personal care when there may be unpleasant odors. The odors should disappear, however, when the soiled linen is discarded into closed containers. Facilities with pervasive odors may have many residents who are not being given incontinent care in a timely manner. I've given many tours of my nursing home to potential families; almost always, at the end of the tour, a family member says, "Gosh! It doesn't smell like urine in here."

In the beginning, I felt insulted. After all, we work hard to care for our residents. Why should it smell like urine? People have preconceived notions about nursing homes, either from visits in the past to grandparents when facilities did smell like urine and did not always offer competent care, or from listening to horror stories from friends. I understand now why people say what they do, and I just chuckle to myself when I hear the "it doesn't smell like urine" line. For the most part, nursing homes offer very good care. There are some facilities that do not offer such care, however, and it is your job to weed them out, if you can.

Look at the building when you are touring. The building and surroundings should be in good repair, clean, and well organized. Don't be misled by a beautiful, plush building, however. An older building with caring, competent staff is much better than a fancy building with a poorly trained, uncaring staff. Care for the elderly is very staff-intensive and doesn't require much technology. Good facilities are good because of the people who work in them, not because of the building that houses them or the fancy brochure that describes them. As a matter of fact, I've run nursing facilities where I didn't even have a brochure. Residents and families came to live at my center because we cared, communicated, and adopted them as part of our family. We spent the money it would cost for brochures, advertising and fancy building decorations on the residents who lived with us and the staff that gave the care.

Look around at the residents as you walk through the facility. Do they look as though they are actively engaged to whatever extent possible, or are they just sitting in the halls asleep in their wheelchairs? Look to see if residents are properly sitting up and positioned in their beds or chairs. If several of the residents are slumped over or look uncomfortably positioned, this should concern you. See if the patients are well groomed. Is their hair brushed, faces and nails clean? Are they wearing clean, appropriate street clothing or is everyone wearing pajamas or hospital gowns? Check what activities are offered and see if patients are encouraged to participate. Each facility has an activity calendar. Look at the calendar during your visit and see what type of activities are offered. If you visit at 10:00 a.m. and there is an activity in the dining room, check to see if any residents are participating, and look to see if staff members are encouraging participation.

If at all possible, schedule your three visits at different times of the day. Go at lunch time and see how the food looks and tastes. Are people given assistance in eating if they need it, or do trays of uneaten food just sit and get cold? Are meal times supervised, and is the dining room a social place where music and friendly conversation exist? Are special diets offered and followed? Ask the patients and staff how the meals are. In a good facility each meal should be nutritious, appetizing and well presented. Substitutes should also be offered as requested, and residents should be able to choose what they want to eat if possible.

Make an evening visit between the hours of 6:30 and 8:30 p.m. Observe the number and quality of staff on duty, and walk around to see if the patients are still sitting up and asking to go back to bed. Listen for call lights, and find out how long it takes for a staff member to respond. You will get varying levels of comfort, walking around the center in the evening. Someone should appear to be in charge and supervising the staff. If the resident you saw during your lunch visit is sitting in the same position and place in the evening, you may assume that she has not received adequate care during the day.

Your third visit should be on the weekend, when the usual management personnel are not in the facility. Look for the same things you did during the week, and speak to the staff and patients. If you are able to find an alert resident, tell her that you are considering placing a loved one at the facility, and ask her what she thinks. Keep in mind that her response may be influenced by her own perception of her situation, negative attitudes, depression or memory troubles. Ask several residents their opinions in order to get a good, overall picture. Most residents will enjoy the chance to meet someone new and have a discussion with a stranger. It may even be helpful to get to know some of the residents during this visit and ask them to befriend your parent when she arrives.

As you do your walk through, observe the staff to see if they are gentle and kind to the residents. Do they treat the resident like an object or a person? Are privacy and dignity respected? Are residents addressed by name and given time to respond to questions? Do staff members touch residents and comfort them if they need help? Does a staff member ask if you need any help as your walk through the facility? An alert staff should always recognize and assist a stranger in the building.

Keep in mind that nursing home staffs typically do their best to offer quality patient care. They operate under very stringent regulations and receive very low reimbursement from the government to provide care for the elderly. Working under these conditions is difficult, and these difficulties are compounded by this country's shortage of qualified nurses and physicians who want to work in the nursing home setting. Many nursing homes can attract qualified staff only from foreign countries, making language, communication and cultural differences an additional challenge. It takes a very special person to work with the elderly. In the medical hierarchy, nursing homes are considered to be at the bottom, and nurses and physicians feel the peer pressure. No matter what anyone else says, I have observed that some of the best nurses and physicians practice in nursing homes; and it's getting better, as the field of geriatrics becomes more and more a specialized area.

Despite all the tremendous obstacles faced by nursing homes, for the most part nursing homes offer caring, compassionate, quality services. When you look for a nursing home, try to have a positive, trusting attitude so that the people you meet will be comfortable and honest with you. Nothing hurts nursing home staff more than the suspicious family member with a preconceived attitude about how terrible nursing homes are. Thousands of dedicated, hard working nursing home employees devote their lives to helping the elderly with very low pay and little appreciation. Matters are made worse when these employees feel mistrusted and are put down by the public. If you understand the needs of the facility in which you are placing your parent, the facility in turn will understand and help you through a difficult time. In many instances the nursing staff will be a second family to your loved one; trust that is developed early may enhance the relationships that are developed.

Try to meet with the administrator or director of nursing at each nursing home you tour. Usually the philosophy of these two key people filters down through the whole facility. Ask about the type of care offered, cost of care, how the facility is staffed, when visitors are permitted (24 hours per day is the best visiting policy), and what to expect after your loved one is admitted. If necessary, write down your questions so that you are prepared. The personnel of all the homes you visit are going to say that they are great, so when you visit nursing home A, question the administrator, director of nurses or—even better—a nursing aide who is the hands-on care provider. Ask what makes their nursing home better then nursing home B or C around the corner. The hands-on employee, such as the nursing aide or housekeeper, will be able to give you an honest, informed answer, since many of these employees work in one or more facilities at a time or have worked previously in several facilities in the area. The nursing aide will tell you if the facility you are visiting is understaffed, without supplies, or of poor quality in service to patients. The nursing aide will also be able to tell you if there is plenty of help, good food, and a kind spirit among patients, staff and management.

As with any other decision you make for your elderly parent, you should use common sense, gut feelings and persistence in gathering and interpreting information. Once you have located a facility with which you and your elderly parent are comfortable, the admission process begins. The nursing home industry is very sensitive to supply and demand. Some areas in the country have too many beds, and some areas have too few beds. You may find a facility that you want, then when it comes time to admit your parent, there may be no bed available. When you are looking, be sure to investigate several; pick the best two or three, in case your first choice has no available beds.

The unfortunate and often unfair aspect of nursing home placement is that, in many instances, the nursing home only wants to admit patients who are easy to care for and paying privately. Patients who need a lot of care and are on Medicaid (MediCal in California) are less desirable, and they may have limited access to available beds. Short term rehabilitation patients are also desirable for some facilities, and these types of patients may gain admission advantage. How you pay for the care your parent will receive may, in fact, determine whether you can get a bed in a desirable facility.

Many caregivers mistakenly believe that Medicare pays for extended nursing home care, so they do not plan ahead. On the contrary, Medicare pays for very little in the nursing home. Medicare pays for nursing home care only if the patient meets certain criteria. If your elderly parent carries Medicare Part A insurance, she can get up to 100 days of nursing home care if there was a three-day hospital stay prior to the nursing home admission and if there is a diagnosis that requires skilled nursing. Medicare sets guidelines for facilities as to what is a covered diagnosis and how long Medicare will pay for the stay. Medicare-covered services may include care in the nursing home after a hip fracture or a stroke. Other skilled services that may allow Medicare coverage in the nursing home include administration of intravenous medication and tube feeding. Each facility has a Medicare utilization review committee that will determine how much coverage will be granted. The first twenty days of Medicare benefits covers the total cost of care in the nursing home. From days 21 to 100, the patient has to pay the nursing home an $84.50 (1993) co-insurance payment. Before your loved one is admitted to the nursing home, you should ask the nursing home representative if your elderly parent will receive Medicare benefits and how long the benefits will last. Make sure you know in advance and are given notice prior to termination of the Medicare coverage, so you can plan for discharge or alternative payment.

If your elderly parent doesn't qualify for Medicare coverage or after benefits are exhausted, there are six other ways to pay for nursing home care.

1. You can pay privately, at a cost that can range between twenty-five and fifty thousand dollars per year.

2. If your elderly parent meets the financial criteria, Medicaid (MediCal in California) may pay the nursing home bill, along with the patient's share of cost.

3. If your elderly parent has long term care insurance, the purchased policy may pay for all or some of the care at the nursing home.

4. If your elderly parent is enrolled in a Medicare HMO such

as FHP, Kaiser, or Secure Horizons, she may be entitled to some skilled nursing or long-term care benefits.

5. If your elderly parent lives in a continuing care retirement community, there should be a health care benefit at the (CCRC) health center.

6. If your elderly parent is a veteran with allowable benefits for long-term care, he may qualify to be in a VA nursing home.

Medicaid is a public assistance program that is granted to low income people based on financial need. Medicaid benefits may be different from state to state, so it is important that you investigate the criteria in the state in which your parent resides. Do your investigating long before a nursing home stay is necessary; by doing so, you may protect your parent's assets and your potential inheritance. I strongly urge all families to get the professional advice of an estate planner or elder-law attorney in order to protect assets and still qualify for Medicaid in time of need.

Children should take a moment to think of how much money they could possibly contribute to the care of their dependent parents, should the need for a nursing home arise. One child may have plenty of extra money to spare, while another may still be financially dependent upon the elderly parent and barely be making ends meet. It's a scary thought to have to give up everything one has to pay for nursing home care. Perhaps if the children all got together and paid the premium on a long term care insurance policy, a financial catastrophe could be avoided.

Nursing home insurance may be a good idea for your family, but be very cautious when you make the purchase. Be sure to ask questions and read the policy completely before signing. Ask specifically what type of care is covered in the policy. Some policies cover only "skilled nursing care" after an acute illness or three-day hospital stay. This type of policy does not provide much benefit to the holder when a long term nursing home stay is required. Most nursing home care is considered "custodial" in nature, for long-term care needed in basic activities such as dressing, bathing, toileting, and eating. Be sure that the policy you purchase specifically covers this type of "custodial" care. Ask if the policy excludes any specific illness or problem, such as Alzheimer's disease. Good policies should not exclude any conditions for coverage. Also get specific answers as to what, if any, preexisting conditions are not covered and for what time frame the coverage is excluded. Be sure to ask these questions and to see the answers in writing.

After you determine specifically what type of care is covered and what illnesses are excluded, ask if a three-day hospital stay is necessary before coverage begins. Find out how long the policy pays, as well as how much it will pay per day for care. The average stay in a nursing home is well over a year, so your policy should provide you with liberal or unlimited benefits. Because most nursing homes charge anywhere from $60.00 to $130.00 per day for care, you should be sure that the daily payment made by the policy is in line with the costs of nursing homes in your area. Also check to see if the daily payment made to the nursing home is fixed or increases if the nursing home raises its rates. You should also determine if there is a waiting period of thirty, sixty or even ninety days after admission before benefits begin. Some policies require such waiting periods so that short nursing home stays may not be reimbursed. If you are concerned about the long term financial impact of care, than a short waiting period may be acceptable to you. Look specifically at the long term care insurance policy to see if it can be canceled by the insurance company for any reason or if your rates can be raised should an illness occur. The best policies will protect holders from cancellation and unfair rate increases. Be aware that a policy is as good as the company that issues it. Check with your insurance commission to see if the company from which you are purchasing the policy is financially solvent and honest about paying claims. Long term care insurance is still a new concept, so pay the extra money and go with an established, well known insurance company.

A lot has been discussed so far in this chapter. We've gotten through the hospital, determined that a nursing home stay is necessary, investigated and chosen a nursing home, and (we hope) figured out how to plan to pay for it. The tough part is yet to come. Admission and adjustment to the facility is a tremendous challenge that requires lots of love, patience and communication.

Every patient admitted to a nursing home needs to be under the care of a physician chosen by the patient or family. The physician is responsible for doing an initial history and physical examination of the patient within the first forty-eight hours of admission and supervising the care thereafter. Unlike the acute care hospital, where patients are seen by the physician each day, in the nursing home the physician is only required to visit once per month. If your loved one has a physician treating her at home or in the hospital, ask up front if he will go to the nursing home to visit. Many physicians simply can't or won't take the time to practice in nursing homes because of the poor reimbursement, time restraints and possible distance of the nursing home from their office practices. This lack of physician participation can compromise continuity and quality of patient care. It is important, therefore, to ask the attending physician whether he will do follow-up care in the nursing home. If he won't, ask him for a referral of a physician who will. It is difficult for an elderly patient who has been seeing one physician for several years to end the relationship and start over. Many doctors are sensitive to this and will make exceptions when it comes to patients with whom they have had long standing relationships. Don't be afraid to ask and push the issue, if the physician doesn't want to follow. If nothing else, ask the physician who knows your elderly parent to call the new physician to discuss the treatment plan. The physicians who practice in nursing homes may also be a valuable resource as to which home is the best, so ask their opinions about the homes you have visited in the area.

Once a physician has been chosen, it is important that you and your elderly parent meet with him/her to discuss care needs, rehabilitation potential, prognosis, treatment plans, and intensity of care issues. I will stress throughout this book that caregivers should allow as much autonomy and participation from their parent as possible. As caregivers, we tend to do the talking for our elderly loved ones, assuming that what we want for them is what they actually want for themselves. Also, our elderly parents sometimes respond in a way that they think will please their adult children, because they want to do the right thing and don't want to be perceived as a burden. Open communication is usually the most effective way to cope with the nursing home experience. Tell your parent what to expect and what all of the options are. Don't be afraid to discuss your feelings as a caregiver, either. I've worked with families that know from the first day of admitting a parent to the nursing home, that she will never be discharged to go back home. The children are afraid to confront the issue, and on each visit, the parent asks when she is going home. The adult child will respond by saying something like, "You can go home, Mom, as soon as you get a little stronger." Mom tries her best to get stronger, with false hopes of returning home. Before long, Mom is angry and discouraged because she is still in the nursing home; the adult child feels guilty and frustrated, because she hasn't effectively and honestly dealt with Mom about the permanent placement issue. Imagining a conversation may help you to be honest and open with your parent about what is going to happen.

"Mom, we've been talking a lot over the past few days about your going to the nursing center tomorrow. It's the center that we talked about and visited. All of us know that this is going to be a challenge, but we all love you and will be with you every step of the way. How do you feel about the move?"

"How should I feel? Of course I want to stay at home. All of you kids think you know what's best for me, so I'll just do as you say."

"Mom, we understand that you want to stay at home. We'd love to have you stay here if it were possible. It's very difficult for you to stay alone, and we're not able to have someone stay with you twenty-four hours a day. For your health and safety, the nursing center is the best place to be. It sounds as if you feel that we're making decisions for you when you could make them for yourself, but we're doing everything we can to give you choices and let you direct your future needs. You always raised us to make tough decisions and follow through, no matter how difficult. This is a tough decision for all of us, and we'll get through it."

"I guess I did raise you like that, didn't I?"

"Yes, you did, and we're glad you did."

"What if I get to the nursing home and decide I don't like it?"

"Well Mom, I'm sure there will be some things you won't like and some things you will like. The place we chose has a caring staff, and they seem to respect all the residents. If we're patient and open minded, we can overcome the negatives. What do you think you won't like about the nursing home?"

"Well, for one thing, I've never shared a room with anyone but your father, and now I'll be sharing with a total stranger. You know how I like to get something to eat whenever I want. Now I'll have to eat when the nursing home serves meals. What if I don't like the food? I have a terrible time sleeping at night. What if I can't sleep? When I have pain in my back and legs, I can take a pain pill whenever I want. I'll bet that at the nursing home I'll have to ask the nurse for a pill when I want one. What if they don't bring me my pills or answer my call when I have to go to the bathroom?"

"Mom, all of your concerns are legitimate, and I'm glad you're sharing them with me. It will be difficult sharing a room with a stranger, but after a few weeks your roommate won't be a stranger anymore. As a matter of fact, you may develop a good friend out of all this. I talked to the social worker at the nursing center, and she said they'd do their best to find you a roommate with similar interests. If you don't like your roommate, we'll find another one. Besides, we're hoping that you won't spend all your time in your room, as you do at home. You can go out for visits with us and participate in activities at the nursing center. When you're in your room, you can always draw the privacy curtain if you want visual privacy. Since you've been sick, we've had to arrange for people to stay with you at home anyway. You didn't like strangers at home because they disrupted your privacy. Unfortunately, we may have to exchange a bit of your privacy in order to get the care and help that you need. You have rights in the nursing center. Respect for your privacy and dignity is something that the nursing home staff is well aware of. If some of them aren't aware, we can teach them what you want and expect. It will take time for the staff to learn your needs and for you to understand what they can provide. As far as your eating whenever you want, well one of the reasons we are concerned about you is because you don't eat right. You eat whatever can be prepared easily, even if it's junk food. The meals that your home caregiver prepared for you weren't as nutritious as the nursing home meals will be. We can bring you all the snacks you want and even put a little refrigerator in your room. The nursing home staff will give you substitutions if you don't like what's on the menu. If you want something from outside, just let the kids know. We can bring you a taco or some pizza when we visit. We can even take you out in the wheelchair. Getting your sleep at night is very important, but you aren't sleeping all night here at home because you nap all day and depend upon a sleeping pill at night. I think those sleeping pills you're taking are having the reverse effect and making you drowsy during the day. Maybe if you get some walking therapy and participate in activities at the nursing center, you will sleep better at night. The doctor says you are taking too many pain pills, and that's why you're constipated and can't concentrate. We're going to see if some therapy at the nursing center will help your back pain, and maybe we can reduce the number of pills you take. If you want to keep your pills at the bedside, I think you can if they are locked up. It may be better for the nurse to give them to you the way the doctor has prescribed. Let's see how it works. We can always make adjustments if necessary."

"Honey, I know you want what's best for me. You're a wonderful daughter, and you go way beyond the call of duty. I'm just afraid that once I'm in the nursing home I'll be forgotten, because the children won't need to actually be there to give me physical care."

"Mom, you're a wonderful mother! How could we forget you? We'll have better times, now. At the nursing center, we'll be able to spend better time with you, because we won't have to be arranging and worrying. We'll know you're safe. You'll have a phone in your room, so you can call us. We'll visit as much as possible, and the visits won't be emergencies, with us feeling stressed because we had to leave work to come help you when your home aide didn't show up. We won't get calls at two in the morning, anymore, hearing a paramedic say that you fell and they had to pick you up and put you back to bed. You'll be in a safe, caring environment at this nursing center. We looked around for quite a while before we found this place, and we had to wait even longer until they had a bed available for you. We'll all work together. I really believe that things will be better. Just remember, Mom, that we want you to share your feelings with us.

We'll do the same with you, and we'll be there to help you through this change."

Pre-admission conversations like this one help ease the initial transition into the nursing home. Adjustment is a process that can take varied amounts of time, depending on an individual's coping skills, as well as the support given by family, friends and nursing home staff.

After choosing the nursing home and preparing your loved one for admission, the actual move must take place. If your loved one is in the hospital, she will probably be transferred from the hospital to the nursing home by ambulance. The ambulance driver will bring copies of medical records and orders from the physician. Usually the hospital discharge planner arranges the time of transport; it is helpful if a family member can be at the hospital to help sign out the patient. Hearing aides, dentures, glasses, and clothes tend to get lost in the transition, so you should check to make sure that the hospital room, drawers and closets are empty upon discharge. If possible, be at the nursing home when your loved one arrives so that she sees a familiar face. If you can go prior to admission and help prepare the nursing home room with familiar possessions, this also helps the transition. Be sure that everything you bring into the nursing home—including clothing, dentures, hearing aides, walkers, and eye glasses—is marked in permanent ink and clearly documented on the patient valuable list. I don't advise that you bring anything expensive, because things may get lost.

At some point in the admission process you will be asked to sign the admission papers. If your loved one is capable of signing these papers, it would be wise to have her do this so that you assume no responsibility. If you have a durable power of attorney for health care or are the conservator for your loved one, you may be the logical one to sign the admission papers. Just remember that you are signing and entering into a contractual arrangement. This agreement sets forth not only the responsibilities to be carried out by the facility, but also the obligations taken on by the resident or resident's responsible party. Make sure that you understand what you are signing. If you don't understand, ask questions. If you sign as the responsible party for your loved one, you may be obligated to pay the bill. If your loved one is on Medicaid (MediCal in California), it is illegal to make someone other than the resident sign as the responsible party. Be sure to ask what your personal liability is if your loved one's money runs out. Also ask if the facility participates in Medicaid (MediCal). If it doesn't, you must be sure that there are adequate resources to pay for care; if there are none, your loved one may be asked to leave when the money runs out. Don't wait until all of the assets are exhausted before you think about moving your loved one from a facility that doesn't participate in Medicaid to one that does. Chances are it will be difficult to find a bed in a Medicaid facility if you don't pay privately for some period of time. If you are admitted to a Medicaid-participating facility, you cannot be discharged if you convert from private pay to Medicaid. You should receive a bill of rights when you enter a facility; these statements delineate what rights your loved one has as a resident of a long term care facility. Read those rights and explain them to your loved one. They include the right to:

- be informed of services available and charges for those services;
- be informed of your medical condition and diagnosis;
- refuse treatment;
- participate in the planning of your care;
- not be discharged without an appropriate reason;
- manage your financial affairs or be given an accounting of financial transactions made on your behalf;
- be free from mental and physical abuse;
- be free from physical and chemical restraints;
- have confidential treatment;
- be treated with dignity and privacy;
- associate and communicate privately with anyone you wish;
- participate with any group;
- retain personal possessions;
- have visitors without interference;
- have access to a telephone and make confidential calls;
- purchase drugs and medical supplies from the pharmacy of your choice.

Resident rights are extremely important and are highly respected in well run nursing facilities. As caregivers, we need to see that our loved one's rights are not being violated. Getting to know the staff at the nursing home and watching interaction between staff and our loved one will give us indications if rights are being respected. If you see a problem with rights not being respected, this should be brought to the attention of the facility administration.

Once you read the admission contract and sign all the paper work, it is time to settle in. I have always believed it to be important to explain to residents and families what to expect and how things in a nursing home work. If you understand a little bit about the operation of the facility, you will know better how to solve potential problems. To better understand how a nursing home operates, it is helpful to know a little bit about the organization of departments.

Each facility has a nursing department that is managed by a **director of nursing**. The director of nursing is responsible for the overall management of the nursing department and may be a good person for you to know, should you have any concerns about your loved one's care.

The dietary department is managed by a **dietary supervisor or dietitian** who oversees the food service for the residents. Any questions or concerns about diets or meals should be directed to the food service supervisor.

Most facilities have a **housekeeping and laundry supervisor**, who may be able to help you with concerns about laundering clothes or cleaning the room of your loved one.

The **activity director** of the nursing center is in charge of meeting the recreational needs of the residents and can assist your loved one in keeping actively involved with meaningful activities.

The **social service worker** in a facility is responsible for meeting the resident's and family's psycho-social needs. If you have concerns about your loved one's behavior or emotional well-being, it would be helpful to speak with the facility's social service worker. The social service worker may also be instrumental in helping the resident adapt to the new living arrangement, as well as arranging for discharge home.

The **bookkeeper** is a good person to know if you have questions about bills or charges you receive during a nursing home stay. The bookkeeper may help you with questions regarding Medicare, Medicaid or insurance billing.

The **administrator** of the nursing home is responsible for the total operation of the facility and should be able to assist you with any of your questions or concerns. Most administrators are happy to help families in any way possible, especially if questions or problems are not resolved by the facility staff.

Day to day care will be given to your loved one by a **nursing assistant**. The nursing assistant is the backbone of the nursing center and is the staff person who usually does the hands-on care of feeding, dressing, bathing, and changing incontinent patients. If your loved one has certain patterns or rituals, it would be helpful to share these with the nursing assistant rendering care. Many times the family has been able to manage certain problems at home through trial and error. Sharing this information with the nursing staff will be very helpful.

The **licensed registered or practical nurses** are responsible for administering medications and treatments for your loved one and assessing any nursing or medical needs. If you have questions about what the doctor has ordered, the licensed nurse will be able to answer you.

Many facilities offer physical, occupational and speech therapy to those who qualify for rehabilitation services. Medicare may cover these services if there is a diagnosis that warrants the skills of a licensed therapist. Ask the nursing director if therapy will be covered by Medicare, and ask the doctor if it should be ordered.

The **physical therapist** works with patients to restore functions lost through strokes, fractures or other debilitating diseases.

The **occupational therapist** may assist the patient with relearning dressing, grooming, eating or other lost living skills.

The **speech therapist** helps the resident to regain speech and comprehension after a stroke or brain injury.

Even if your loved one is not entitled to therapy services, at a minimum you can request that a restorative nursing program be followed. The restorative program is carried out by the nursing staff and insures that your loved one is helped to walk daily and given range of motion exercises to prevent muscle atrophy and contractures.

As you get more familiar with the nursing home, you will know whom to ask for what information. I would request an orientation to staff and programs, if it isn't offered as part of the entrance routine. You would also do well to request that you and your loved one meet with the nursing home staff to go over what type of care and services are necessary. If you anticipate a long term stay, you should also request a quarterly meeting with staff to determine how things are going.

You and your elderly parent will still face many challenges, even after her admission to a nursing home. Many adult children mistakenly believe that the burden they experienced as caregivers will disappear once their parent is admitted to the nursing home. The perceived burden doesn't always go away. It does change, however. You must let go and learn to trust the nursing home staff to care for your parent. Your parent will also have to trust strangers to meet her needs. At times, you may find yourself having to solve problems or resolve your parent's complaints about her living arrangements. I encourage families to assist their parent in solving problems and maintaining autonomy as much as possible. We tend at times to do too much for our parent out of love and concern. Doing too much may lead to an excessive amount of dependence on your parent's part and leave her without the ability to solve problems on her own in your absence.

Even in the best nursing home, you should be aware of potential problems and challenges that are common to the elderly in institutional environments. Your extra set of eyes and involvement may be of great assistance to your parent. Be sensitive to the feelings of the staff and your parent when making suggestions. If the staff perceives you as interfering with care and being bossy, they may not respond favorably to your inquiries. If the staff perceives you as supportive and concerned, you may be more successful in your dealings with them.

Some common problems and challenges inherent to life in a nursing home include:

- falls and the use of restraints;
- use of medication;
- dehydration;
- unnecessary and excessive immobility;
- problem behaviors;
- skin care;
- loss of appetite and weight;
- anxiety and depression;
- relationships with staff and other residents;
- loss of independence in activity of daily living skills;
- recognizing condition changes;
- communication;
- loss of personal belongings; and
- life and death decisions.

Many of these problems and challenges are discussed at length in other chapters of this book. I shall briefly cover some of these topics as they relate to care in the nursing home. Again I emphasize that acquiring knowledge and planning ahead may be the most valuable steps you take. Learning about these issues now may prevent problems in the future.

Now Mom or Dad is admitted to the nursing home. What is next? The caregiving mission continues, much to the dismay of many caregivers. Nursing homes can be good places if they are properly operated and managed. By paying heed to the section on choosing a nursing home, you have selected a better than average place for your elderly parent to live. Your goals as a caring child should not change. Even if your elderly parent will not get much better, it is important to help her to adjust and gain some quality of life in her new living arrangement. At some point in the nursing home experience, you will be asked to make decisions about issues or will be informed of your elderly parent's condition. If you have a durable power of attorney for health care, let the facility know and give them a copy. Durable power of attorney is discussed in Chapter 29.

It's likely that you may need to have a discussion about falls and the use of restraints. Elderly people at home and in institutions fall; life threatening injuries may result. Nursing homes, like other institutions, do not want to be liable if your parent falls and gets hurt in the facility. The first reaction after a fall or suspected fall may be to have your parent restrained in the wheelchair or bed. **It is your parent's right not to be restrained, and you should be assertive in seeing that this right is not violated if your parent cannot speak for herself.**

The difficulty with restraints is that they cause excess immobility and dependence upon staff. A person restrained in a wheelchair who wants to use the bathroom is out of luck if nobody wants to help or if nobody is around. The problem of immobility is terrible in a frail, elderly individual. If one is restrained in a wheelchair and not helped to walk regularly, it's not too long before the muscles atrophy and the individual actually can't walk anymore. Restraints may also contribute to excess agitation, irritability, and depression.

So what do you do if you get a call from the nursing home saying that Mom has fallen and they want to restrain her? Or worse yet, what do you do if you visit one day and find Mom in a restraint (postural support) and nobody even asked you or her if it was O.K.? The first thing you do is call a meeting with your parent and the charge nurse to discuss the benefits and risks of restraint use. The goal of this meeting will be to figure out the least restrictive measure that will provide safety for your parent and not significantly reduce the quality of her life. If she is falling, she should be evaluated as to possible reasons and reversible causes. This type of evaluation is discussed in Chapter 4.

Excessive medications, chronic illness, disorders of gait, dementia, and environmental barriers all contribute to falls in the nursing home. Many falls occur there when the patient is trying to get from bed to the bathroom. With a regular toileting program, perhaps these types of falls can be avoided. If your loved one can be reminded to keep the call light within reach and to call for help, perhaps the risk of falling will be reduced.

Actually, many nursing home staff members take a paradoxical approach to managing potential falls. When a patient falls they put her in a restraint that restricts mobility and lessens the ability to walk. Instead of restraining the patient, they should offer walking therapy so that muscles are strengthened and walking ability is improved. Before you allow your loved one to be restrained—unless it is a temporary emergency—you should have the physician, physical therapist and nursing staff do a complete evaluation and provide an alternate treatment plan. Some alternatives to restraints include velcro seat belts, special pillows, and bed and wheelchair alarms that are activated when the patient's weight is lifted from the sensor. If it is decided after a complete evaluation that your elderly parent needs to be restrained to protect her health and safety, then her care should be monitored to insure that the restraints are released at a minimum of one time every two hours. She should be taken to the bathroom, turned in bed, and given range of motion exercises. If you are not sure whether restraints are being released, you can check by using a technique that I have used as an administrator to be sure that my patients are given the care they need. During your visit, take a pen and mark with ink on the top of the knot where the restraint is tied. Come back in a couple of hours or later in the day and see if the mark is in the same place on the restraint. If it is, the restraint was not untied and your parent was not repositioned. Remember that your parent has the right to be free from physical restraints. The decision should be made with input from your parent, the family, and the health care team. The need for restraints should be evaluated regularly to see if they are still necessary, and the utmost care should be given to see that there is no unnecessary physical or emotional decline as a result of restraints. Bed rails are also restraints, but they are considered less restrictive. They may keep your parent from rolling out of bed; they may also contribute to falls, however, if your loved one can't easily exit the bed and decides to scoot to the foot of the bed and over the foot board. Falling over the side rails can be more harmful, because the patient is falling from a higher point. Similar evaluations should be done to determine whether side rails are necessary. When decisions about restraints are required, quality of life should be considered. Perhaps it is better to risk the chance of falling in exchange for independence. These are difficult decisions that require a tremendous amount of courage and conviction on everyone's part. You will know that you have done your job as a caregiver if all alternatives to restraints are investigated and if the decision to restrain is done with the best interest of your parent in mind—not for the convenience of nursing home staff or fear of liability.

The use of medication in the nursing home should be monitored very closely by the caregiver. Chapter 6 covers in detail what you should know. The average nursing home resident may take six or more medications at one time. You should know and keep a list of what your loved one is taking, and ask to be informed when anything new is added to the medication regimen. Every medication should have a diagnosis that justifies its use, and each medication should have a duration of treatment that is regularly evaluated to determine if the medication is still necessary. If your loved one has any acute change in mental abilities or physical functioning, the first thing you should suggest to the nursing home staff is to evaluate the medications she is taking. It may even be helpful to suggest to the physician that a drug holiday be declared, discontinuing medications under supervision, to see if the patient's condition improves. As a general rule, the fewer the medications, the better off your loved one will be. Be careful to note any changes in condition that are associated with the addition of new medicine or the discontinuing of existing medication. You may be the first to notice changes in your elderly parent. Of course you hope that problems are picked up by alert nursing home staff and that you aren't the first to notice. If you learn nothing else, however, you should keep in mind that medication problems can cause significant difficulty for the elderly nursing home patient. Be aware, and bring any potential problems to the attention of the nursing home staff.

Anxiety and depression are emotional states that are quite prevalent in the nursing home population. Signs and symptoms of these problems may include irritability, changes in appetite, difficulty sleeping, fatigue, difficulty concentrating, loss of interest in normal activities and physical complaints such as pain, headache, muscle tension, palpitations, difficulty breathing, and even constipation. Because depression is such a major problem in the elderly, I have devoted a complete chapter to evaluation and treatment (Chapter 5). Just recognizing the signs of depression and developing a treatment plan with the nursing home staff may be life saving for your parent.

At the most basic level, you should assist your parent in making certain that her physical and emotional needs are being met in the nursing home. Something as simple as not drinking enough water can be life threatening if your parent does not receive adequate amounts of fluids daily. Any number of factors in the nursing home may contribute to dehydration, which can be life threatening. Be sure that your parent has access to water and is given water regularly by staff. You should also encourage her to drink during your visits, unless there is a fluid restriction ordered by the physician.

Basic needs, such as going to the bathroom, may also have to be monitored in the nursing home. If your parent is limited physically and takes a long time to walk to the bathroom and get on and off the toilet, there may be a tendency on the part of the busy nursing home staff to put an adult diaper on her. No patient should be forced to wear a diaper because of time restraints of the nursing home staff. Incontinence (involuntary loss of urine or feces) is discussed in detail in Chapter 17. Read the section on incontinence and apply it to the nursing home experience. If your parent enters the nursing home without needing diapers, you should insist on a thorough evaluation before diaper use is instituted. Adult diapers do have their place in the care of a nursing home patient who has no voluntary control of urine. If used to keep patients clean and dry between regular toileting, the diapers can be a life saver. If not used for this purpose, they can foster dependence, regression and humiliation. One of the most humiliating things you can hear a nursing home staff member say to an elderly patient when she asks to go to the bathroom is: "It's O.K. to go in your diaper." I care tremendously about my patients, and I have actually brought adult disposable diapers home to try on myself in order to see which is the most comfortable for my patients. When I tried to void in the diaper, I just couldn't bring myself to do it. Like restraint use, the use of diapers for incontinence has its place if proper evaluation and alternative measures are instituted. As soon as someone on the nursing staff recommends diapers for your parent who was never before incontinent, ask for a meeting and question why. If incontinence is temporary, due to drugs or urinary tract infection, be sure that the diaper use is discontinued after the acute problem is resolved. You can also request that your parent be put on a bowel and bladder retraining program, in which toileting is scheduled and progress towards continence is monitored. A final note on incontinence relates to the use of foley catheters. A foley catheter is a tube that is placed in the urethra that leads to the bladder. The tube drains urine from the bladder and the urine is collected in a bag at the distal end of the catheter tubing. It is very common for elderly patients to have catheters inserted to measure urine output when they are in the hospital. When the patient is transferred to the nursing home, the catheter may be left in because nobody thinks to take it out or because the nursing home staff assumes the catheter is necessary. If your loved one has a catheter, speak with the doctor to see if it can be removed. Long term catheter use can lead to infection and other adverse problems, and a catheter should only be used if an elderly person is unable to void. Occasionally, catheter use is also warranted if a patient is incontinent and has a pressure sore that will be made worse if irritated by urine, or has a terminal illness or other condition which makes toilet use uncomfortable or very difficult. If your loved one has a catheter, just be sure to check with the doctor and nursing home staff to see if its continued use is warranted.

Another common problem related to physical care in the nursing home is fecal impaction. Simply stated, a fecal impaction is when stool partially or completely blocks the intestine and cannot be passed. Something as simple as this can be life threatening to an elderly nursing home patient whose bowel patterns are not being monitored. If your loved one complains of not having a bowel movement for several days or has diarrhea that is caused by seepage of stool around the impaction, tell the nursing staff. The nursing staff can either manually disimpact the patient or use suppositories and laxatives to help relieve the problem. Symptoms of a fecal impaction may include abdominal pain and cramping, fever, diarrhea, transitory urinary incontinence, nausea and vomiting. If your loved one develops these symptoms in the nursing home, ask that she be checked for a fecal impaction before she is rushed to the hospital. It sounds strange that you should need to do something so simple as monitor your loved one's bowel and bladder habits, but it may be necessary.

This chapter was not intended to paint a bleak picture of nursing homes and the care offered in them. The nursing home may be the correct arrangement for your loved one, and the care she receives can be outstanding.

You can improve relations by occasionally bringing goodies and treats for the nursing home staff to recognize their hard work. Give a nurse a compliment and a pat on the back sometimes. Volunteer your time to help with activities, if you can. The more you accept the situation and get positively involved, the more your parent may follow your example.

You do, however, want to talk to the administrator if your parent is complaining about rough treatment. When dealing with grievances, assure your loved one that she can express herself without fear of retaliation. If at all possible, enable her to resolve the problem for herself, so that she doesn't perceive herself as being helpless. With any complaint or concern, ask as an open ended question what the problem is. Let your parent tell the story her way, without interruption. After the story is told, get specifics.

If, for example, your parent complained of being handled roughly, ask such questions as these:

- What part of your body was handled roughly? Describe how you were treated. Pretend that I'm the staff member. Show me what happened.
- Are you hurt now? Where does it hurt? Do you have any bruises?
- What happened right before the incident? What happened after the incident?
- Was anything said to you while this was going on?
- What time did it happen? Was it dark out or light? Was it before dinner or after dinner?
- Do you know the person's name who treated you this way? If not, what did the person look like? How did the person talk?
- Did you report this to anyone on the staff? What was the response?
- Has this happened before?

It is very difficult to determine what is real and what is not real, especially when your parent is suffering from memory loss. I always give my patients the benefit of the doubt, especially when it comes to potentially serious complaints. I have worked in nursing homes for several years and have heard many complaints from many people. Most of the complaints are minor to me, but major to someone who is ill, dependent and confined to a nursing home. For this reason I treat every complaint or concern with respect, and I investigate and help as much as possible. Many complaints are unfounded, some are real and can be corrected, and still others are real and must be lived with and accepted as part of institutional living. Our job as caregivers is to help our elderly parents in nursing homes deal with and address issues that are distressing in their lives. Dealing effectively does not necessarily, however, mean that you have to be bombarded with complaints every time you visit. You need to set boundaries with your parent so that you do not spend all of your visit dealing with chronic complaints that you can do nothing about. You will burn out and will no longer want to visit. When you stop visiting, your parent will complain that you don't visit enough. If your parent chronically complains, you may not be able to change this behavior. Complaining may be a result of anger about placement or frustration about dependence. Perhaps discussing these feelings with your parent may help. If you are uncomfortable and unhappy about having your parent in the nursing home, your feelings may be evident in your parent's attitude toward placement.

As a caregiver and a child, you may feel guilty or unfaithful for placing your parent in a nursing home. After all, if your parents cared for you through thick and thin, why can't you return the favor? Don't be so hard on yourself. If you can't actually care for your elderly parent in your home, you still can be actively involved in her care at the nursing home. Your lack of physical presence does not in any way diminish your love and commitment to your parent. You can still be there for each other, even if you are not living in the same home. I trust that after reading this chapter the hospital and nursing home experience will be a little bit easier to manage. If you have gained nothing else, at least you will know where to go, how to get there, and what to do once you have arrived.

13

INTRODUCTION TO COMMON MEDICAL PROBLEMS AND FUNCTIONAL DECLINES IN THE ELDERLY

ONE OF THE MOST PRECIOUS GIFTS WE HAVE is our health, and many of us don't realize this until our health fails us. As we get older our bodies change, and we are often faced with chronic illnesses affecting our ability to function on a daily basis. The goal of the caregiver and health care provider thus changes from cure to maintaining functional abilities. In other words, if your elderly parent suffers from arthritis, it is doubtful that the problem can be cured. The goal is to reduce pain, maintain mobility, and assist your elderly loved one to function independently in her environment.

Because of the nature of problems experienced by the elderly, it is necessary for caregivers, elderly patients, and physicians to work closely as a team. You as a caregiver may have to take an active role in the health care of your elderly parent, especially if she cannot access the care that is needed or does not comply with the treatment that is suggested. Finding the appropriate physician is very important, because some physicians don't find working with the elderly rewarding. It takes quite a bit of time to assess and address the concerns of elderly patients and their families because of the multifactorial nature of the problems. To merely get an elderly patient in and out of the office and on and off the exam table, in addition to obtaining a reliable history, takes much more time than it would for a younger patient. Also, because many elderly patients have several chronic illnesses that need attention, the physician must take much more time to do the proper assessment and make the appropriate recommendations. Geriatrics (the care of the elderly) is slowly becoming a specialized field of medicine, and there are now some doctors who are board certified and specializing in this field. If you could find such a doctor, it would be great. If not, a good family physician or internist who is willing to spend time with you and your elderly loved one would be acceptable.

The body is a complex system of chemicals, cells, organs, and organ systems that interact at multiple levels. The following chapters are meant to serve as a simplified overview of how the different organs and systems in the body change and are affected by disease. We recognize in pediatrics that a child is not just a smaller version of an adult who requires similar assessments and treatments. The same is true in geriatrics. An older adult does not always respond in the same way to disease or stress as a younger or middle-aged adult.

Some basic knowledge of common diseases and disorders of the elderly will assist caregivers to make informed decisions and practice preventive health care with their elderly loved ones. Some very important principles are crucial for caregivers of the elderly to understand. The first principle is that **diseases and illnesses sometimes appear with different symptoms in the elderly than they do in the young.** Many times the onset of a serious illness will show up as poor appetite, weakness, falls, confusion, lethargy, fatigue, agitation, changes in behavior, or what we call just failure to thrive. Older people may have a limited reserve of strength and function, and a problem in one body system may surface with symptoms in an unsuspected area. Early detection and treatment are essential, because the ability to recover may decline as one ages. Keeping these principles in mind, let's explore the common medical problems and declines associated with the later years of life.

14

WHAT TO EXPECT AFTER A STROKE

I got the call at 5:00 a.m. I was curled up under the warm blankets in a twilight sleep, the type of sleep when you know it will be time to awaken soon and wish that you could just stay in bed all day long. As the phone rang my heart jumped, and I could feel it pounding in my chest. My phone never rang at this hour in the morning. It was either a wrong number or something was wrong with Dad. God, how I wish it had been a wrong number. I'm not sure what the person on the line really said. All I remember is the five words, "Your dad had a stroke."

I was scared to death, and after I hung up the phone I got a terrible feeling in the pit of my stomach. I imagined the worst, as I always do. I jumped out of bed, and from that point on, it was like a dream. On the way to the hospital I prepared myself for the bad news. Would Dad die? Would he be left as an invalid? Who would take care of him? Is he going to suffer? Why does this have to be happening to us?

When I arrived at the emergency room, I went to the desk and asked to see my father. After a few minutes the nurse led me to the x-ray department, where she said that dad would be having a brain scan. I walked in the room and looked on the gurney at my dad. He seemed to recognize me, but when he tried to say my name the words wouldn't come out. I could see in his eyes that he was scared, yet happy to see a familiar face. I sat and held his hand, rubbed his forehead, and cried inside. I tried not to show my feelings, because I didn't want to alarm Dad. As I held his hand, I prayed for him.

They took Dad away and asked me to wait in the waiting room. It was about 6:00 a.m. by this time, and the waiting room was the last place I wanted to be. I wanted to be with my dad and talk to the doctor. It was a cold morning, and the waiting room chairs were not very comfortable. They were the type that are in rows of six and bolted to the floor. A security guard and a few other people like me were in the waiting room. They were also waiting for news about loved ones. There was one lady who was sick to her stomach and waiting to see the doctor. She looked worse than I did, but that didn't make me feel any better. I'll always have a picture of those events in my mind. It was sort of like being out of my body and looking down on everything. There was a television set in the corner of the ceiling, and I think there was some morning talk show on. I even remember the smell of the crisp morning air mixed with coffee that the nurses were brewing.

My daydream was shattered as I heard the automatic doors swing open and saw a young man in surgical greens and a white lab coat walk toward me. My heart started racing again. What would the news be? As the doctor got close, I felt a little relieved. He had very kind, tired eyes and he was in desperate need of a shave. For some reason, I felt instantly comfortable with this doctor. It was as though he knew what was happening and that things were going to be just fine. He told me that my dad had had a stroke and that it would be a couple of days before he would know the extent of neurological damage. He said that they were moving Dad to the intensive care unit where they would monitor him very closely.

I had so many questions, but all I could think to ask was, "Will he be all right?" The doctor put his hand on my shoulder and said very honestly that he didn't know. It was the first time I'd ever heard a doctor admit not knowing something. After he left, I looked through my purse to find my brother's phone number. I had not talked with him in months and I certainly didn't want to call him with news like this. I took a deep breath and headed for the pay phone in the lobby of the hospital. This was the day I'd always hoped would never come—the day that my caregiving mission for Dad began. I look back at that day wishing that I'd have been prepared. Perhaps I would have handled things differently. It's been three years of caregiving since the stroke, but I remember it as though it happened this morning. It's been a struggle for Dad and the family. If it had been a wrong number that morning, our lives would be drastically different now.

Everyone dreads a phone call like the one this daughter received. The intent of this chapter is to help prepare the caregiver, in case that 5:00 a.m. call ever comes.

Strokes can be the most devastating of problems faced by the elderly. The issue is equally as devastating for caregivers. If a stroke doesn't cause death, it almost always produces disabilities that require rehabilitation and long term care.

Many people perceive strokes as a homogeneous problem, when in fact there are different causes for strokes and different resultant disabilities in stroke victims. Very basically, a stroke results when the brain does not receive sufficient oxygenated blood in its cells and tissues. Without this blood supply, the cells and tissues of the brain die. The types of disabilities caused by the stroke depend upon where tissue damage of the brain occurs, as well as the extent of the damage that is caused.

There are four common ways for blood supply to the brain

to be interrupted and for strokes to occur. Due to very high blood pressure, a blood vessel in the brain can rupture and disrupt blood flow to the brain tissue, causing swelling and pressure in the brain. These types of strokes are commonly referred to as cerebral hemorrhages, and the results can be quite damaging. Strokes can also be caused by interruption of blood flow to the brain by an occlusion of blood vessels. Usually these occlusions in the blood vessels are caused by atherosclerosis. In some cases, blood vessels in the brain are occluded by a blood clot that travels to the brain from other areas in the body. Strokes can also develop when not enough blood reaches the brain, due to low blood pressure caused by such problems as dehydration and shock. Each different type of stroke may have different symptoms and may cause different types of disabilities. The initial treatment of each stroke, as well as the type and amount of rehabilitation, may also vary according to the cause and result of the stroke.

In some cases early treatment of a stroke may be life saving. In other cases there is no treatment for a stroke at all. As caregivers, prevention is a number one priority. You can assist in prevention by monitoring the medical care of your frail, elderly parent. If you know what symptoms to look for, perhaps you can intervene at an early stage and prevent a catastrophic stroke.

Prior to having a stroke, some people may experience what are called TIAs. TIA stands for transient ischemic attack. It is a fancy name for the supply of blood to the brain being temporarily interrupted, causing temporary neurological changes to occur. Symptoms may include such temporary conditions as loss of consciousness, loss of speech or vision, inability to walk, and paralysis or numbness in one or more extremities. The key word is temporary. With a stroke, there is usually permanent damage. Usually after a TIA, the person regains full neurological function within a brief period of time. If your parent experiences the above mentioned problems, you should initiate a full evaluation by a physician. Many times these conditions can be treated with medication or surgery to prevent a stroke.

You should also be aware of the symptoms of a stroke in progress, so that you can summon help promptly. Symptoms vary in nature and severity, so use the following indications as general guidelines for summoning help:

- severe headache, with or without nausea or vomiting;
- slurred speech or difficulty speaking;
- change in the level of consciousness;
- inability to be aroused;

- loss of coordination or balance;
- sudden inability to walk;
- facial droop or drooling from the side of the mouth;
- inability to move one or more limbs on command;
- changes in vision;
- sudden weakness and inability to sit or stand; or
- sudden loss of bladder or bowel control.

Just being aware of the above symptoms may aide you in early detection of a stroke in progress, so that you can seek prompt medical attention. The hospital and nursing home experience is discussed in Chapter 12. You should read that chapter to help you prepare for and negotiate getting care for your loved one after a stroke.

Stroke care and rehabilitation require cooperation between family members, doctors, nurses, therapists and—most of all—the elderly person who suffered the stroke. A stroke can cause difficulty speaking; paralysis; inability or difficulty swallowing; difficulty dressing, bathing, eating, walking or grooming; incontinence (involuntary loss of urine or stool); changes in mood and behavior, as well as changes in intellectual abilities. Strokes cause permanent damage in the areas of the brain that are responsible for these functions. The goal of rehabilitation is to use what abilities are left to attain the maximum level of independent functioning possible. If function cannot be restored, the goal is to prevent further deterioration and to assist the stroke victim to live and cope with resultant disabilities.

Prevention of another stroke is also very important. Steps should be taken to control high blood pressure, diabetes, heart conditions, disease in the carotid arteries, and other medical conditions that may lead to a stroke. Be sure your parent receives thorough medical evaluation and follow-up after the stroke.

It's common for an elderly person to become depressed after a stroke. This depression may detract from the rehabilitation process. Among the patients with whom I work, those who have supportive families and are motivated to get well usually do better in rehabilitation. In the rehabilitation process, be sure that the family is there to help cheer on the stroke victim. Generally after a stroke that has residual effects, the patient will be transferred to a nursing home for rehabilitation. If not transferred to a nursing home, the patient may go home with therapy and assistance to be provided there.

For general information, you may find it helpful to read Chapters 7 (on home care) and 12 (on nursing homes).

After a stroke, the therapists will want to get your parent mobilized. A physical therapist may assist in her regaining balance, strength and mobility. A speech therapist may assist in overcoming difficulties with speech and processing of information. An occupational therapist or speech therapist may work with difficulties in swallowing. An occupational therapist may work on helping your parent regain or relearn self-care activities, such as dressing, eating, bathing, grooming, cooking, and toileting.

If you can arrange to be at the therapy sessions, I recommend that you make every effort to do so, especially if you plan to take your parent home with you after discharge from the hospital or nursing home. I have even suggested that adult children use a home video camera to tape the therapy sessions. Many of the therapy techniques that are used by professional therapists can be used by family members after discharge to maintain functioning of a parent. That's why the family caregiver should be available to learn and follow through after discharge.

Specific therapy techniques are beyond the scope of this book and really should be taught to the family or patient by the physical, occupational or speech therapist. Actually, each rehabilitation program should be individually tailored to the ability and disability of the patient. The goal of this chapter is to give the reader enough knowledge to ask the right questions.

Some specific problems related to strokes can be addressed with courage and patience. To assist caregivers and patients in coping, the most common difficulties relating to strokes are covered here.

PARALYSIS:

Some strokes cause paralysis on either the left or right side of the body. While the use of a leg or an arm on the affected side of the body may never be fully regained, it is important to follow the therapist's directions as to how to position and passively exercise the limbs. Not using a limb due to paralysis can cause the muscles in the limb to waste away, spasm and contract. If an elderly person has a contracted hand, arm or leg, it is usually due to an after-effect of a stroke. Get actively involved in the rehabilitation process, and have the therapist show you how to assist your parent in exercising and positioning the affected body part. Better yet, if your parent still has use of one side of the body, encourage her to exercise the bad limb with the help of the good limb. Ask the therapist about adaptive equipment available to assist with dressing, eating, bathing and grooming. Adaptive equipment assists the patient in doing daily activities that can no longer be performed independently after the stroke. Built up plates and handles of silverware assist in eating. Special reachers and bathing utensils help with dressing and bathing. There is even equipment available to help button buttons and tie shoes.

Get a catalog of adaptive equipment from the therapist so that you can order what is needed for Mom or Dad. If dressing is a problem, some of this adaptive equipment may not be as necessary if you get simple clothing for Mom or Dad to wear. Ask the therapist for clothing recommendations regarding the best attire. Velcro in place of buttons may help some people get dressed more independently. Remember that the goal of rehabilitation is to help your parent to help herself. If you do everything for her, she may never reach her highest independent functional ability.

Many times, paralysis of body parts after a stroke can lead to pressure ulcers (bedsores). After a stroke, a paralyzed limb may not have feeling in it. If the limb is left in one position for two or more hours, the pressure may cause the blood supply to be interrupted, and an ulcer may develop. Be sure to protect vulnerable parts of immobilized limbs—like the heels and elbows—from pressure by shifting their position at least every two hours. The use of pressure-relieving equipment like heel protectors may also help to prevent bedsores from developing in a paralyzed limb.

COMMUNICATION:

After a stroke, your loved one may have difficulty communicating. It is terribly frustrating to not be able to make one's needs known, especially when one is dependent upon others for care and assistance. When attempting to get thoughts across to your loved one, try to be patient. She may understand you and just not be able to tell you what she wants to say. She may use the wrong words and even say the word *yes* when she means *no*. At times, she may even repeat the same word or phrase over and over again. It helps to talk slowly when you want to communicate with your parent who has suffered a stroke. If she doesn't understand a word or a phrase, try using a different word or phrase that conveys the same meaning. You may even try to write what you are trying to say, if that helps.

Special communication boards are available that have pictures of common requests which someone who can't communicate may try to make. Providing such a board may help alleviate some frustration and allow your loved one to make her needs known. Ask the speech or occupational therapist for a communication board if it isn't provided or suggested by one of them. Let me caution you not to talk in front of your parent as though she isn't there. This is a common error. A stroke victim's confusion or inability to speak or communicate doesn't mean that she can't hear and understand what is going on around her.

EMOTIONAL REACTIONS:

After a stroke, your elderly loved one may experience changes in emotions. She may seem sad or have angry outbursts. She may even seem to cry for no reason. Try to offer as much support as possible, and don't take these outbursts personally. Most of the time this type of behavior is a result of damage to the brain caused by the stroke. It may be helpful to keep track of what happens directly prior to the outbursts. Sometimes you'll be able to find out what, if any, frustrations or upsetting events lead to the problem. Calm reassurance and empathy for the person often help. Redirecting your loved one when these behaviors occur may also alleviate the problem somewhat. It is very difficult to help someone who can't communicate her needs. You may just have to anticipate what the problem or need is and try different interventions until one works.

SWALLOWING AND CHOKING:

After a stroke, your loved one may have difficulty swallowing or clearing secretions. You may feed her and notice that she holds the food in the cheek without swallowing. Difficulties with chewing and swallowing may lead to choking or to aspiration of food and liquid into the lungs. When food or fluid goes into the lungs, the result may be pneumonia. If your loved one is having difficulty chewing or swallowing after a stroke, ask for an evaluation by the doctor and speech therapist if one isn't offered automatically. In order to avoid problems, follow instructions on preparation of food and on assistance in feeding. Sometimes the doctor will order only thickened liquids for your parent. If family members aren't aware of this order, they may inadvertently offer water to the stroke patient and cause choking or aspiration.

In some cases, your elderly parent may not be able to take any food or fluids because of the inability to swallow or because of a decreased level of consciousness. If this happens after a stroke, the doctor may suggest tube feedings. When a stroke patient requires tube feeding, liquid nutrition is provided through a tube that is placed either through the nose, in order to reach the stomach (nasogastric feeding), or directly into the stomach through the abdominal wall (gastric feeding).

Before consenting to such procedures, have extensive conversations with the family and health care team. It helps if you know what your parent's advance wishes were regarding artificial feeding and life prolongation. These issues are discussed in other areas of this book. You must find out the anticipated duration of the tube feedings and the quality of life which can be expected for your parent.

While in practical terms it makes no difference whether a tube feeding is never started or is discontinued, ethically it is often easier *not* to begin tube feeding than to remove a tube after it has been placed. The end result is that your parent will die if she doesn't get an adequate supply of fluids and nutrition. The decision should be based upon what your parent's wishes are, taking into account the quality of life that she will have after the stroke. Many hospitals have bioethics committees that will assist you in such life and death decisions. In addition to asking the physician's advice, you may also request recommendations from such a committee if the matter cannot be resolved.

I can't remind you enough that durable power of attorney documents and advanced directives should be drafted far in advance of a crisis. This is also discussed in Chapter 29. If a tube feeding is initiated, be sure that at home or in the nursing home, the staff are following certain precautions. Such precautions include 1) keeping the head of the bed elevated so that the tube feeding doesn't go into the lungs accidentally and 2) checking to see that the tube is in the stomach before starting the feedings. Learn from the nursing staff so that you know how to look for problems. The key to being a good caregiver, whether you are providing the care or trusting others to do it, is information.

If your parent has a reaction to the tube feeding, speak with the dietitian or physician and see if the feeding can be changed.

There are several tube feeding solutions available that provide complete nutrition. Some are better than others when it comes to patient tolerance. One last note on tube feedings is that often, calorie and fluid needs are not adequately met if the caregiver isn't aware of the requirements. Simply ask how many calories your loved one is receiving with the tube feeding, and find out how the number is calculated. Ask the doctor and dietitian if this number of calories is sufficient. Also see that water is given through the tube if adequate fluids are not being provided with the feeding solution alone.

Few afflictions have more devastating results than strokes. The emotional, physical and financial resources required to care for a stroke victim can be exhausting. In caring for a loved one who has suffered a stroke, you will see that life can change drastically for the caregiver and the one receiving care. Use the information throughout this book to help you cope. Mom or Dad may never fully regain what they once had, but with support and good care, they may be able to maintain and enjoy what still remains.

15

MEMORY LOSS, CONFUSION, ALZHEIMER'S DISEASE

"Mother, where are you going? I just got you dressed and ready for bed."

"I'm going home. Get me my clothes!"

"But Mother, this is your home."

"Nonsense! I'm going home as soon as you find my clothes. Call a taxi."

"Mother, I told you that this is your home. Don't you remember moving here three years ago after Dad died?"

"These damned, thieving people. They are always stealing my clothes. Take me home or I'm calling the police."

The memory loss of a loved one can be a very difficult problem for a caregiver. This vignette illustrates the frustration and stress between a daughter and her memory-impaired mother. How should the caregiver handle this situation? Arguing seems to escalate the anxiety of everyone, and it proves futile in the long run. The daughter knows that it is late; she needs to get some sleep or she will never function at work the next day. Even if she did go to bed, she could only sleep lightly for fear that her mother would get up in the night and wander away looking for "her home."

This scenario played out every night would push even the most patient caregiver over the edge, and often, it does. We will explore in this chapter the problem of memory loss, in an attempt to shed some light on ways to handle difficult behaviors. Because of the progressive nature of memory impairment, it is important to plan ahead and be prepared. You may feel that some issues discussed in this chapter do not apply to you or your situation. Read carefully, however, because you may learn something valuable now that will help you tremendously later.

Probably one of the most devastating problems with which I help families is Alzheimer's disease. As professionals, we consider this disease a family disease because of the effect the patient's condition has on the family system. With other diseases in the elderly, such as heart conditions, arthritis, and even cancer, people generally know what to expect, and in most cases there is treatment available.

With Alzheimer's disease there is no treatment, and families witness their loved one slowly slipping away from them. As the disease progresses, a loved one may no longer recognize a family member as family. Years of love, companionship and history are lost forever.

Scope of the Problem

If your family is affected by Alzheimer's disease or a related disorder, you are not alone. This disease affects more than three million Americans and is the fourth leading cause of death among older people in this country. It is estimated that approximately 10% of those older than 65 suffer from Alzheimer's disease, and 47.2% of those older than 85 are affected. Many people misunderstand the problem and assume that memory loss is a normal consequence of aging. This is a false assumption. There should be no appreciable loss of memory as one ages. Older people may be slower to respond and less interested in the conversation, due to depression or hearing loss; they may even perceive themselves as having poor memory due to aging, when they actually always had a bad memory. I have a terrible memory when it comes to certain things, especially remembering names. If I were eighty years old and I forgot your name, you might label me as being confused or memory impaired, when in fact I probably wouldn't have remembered your name when I was thirty, either.

The public may also be unclear about the various terms used to describe memory loss in the elderly. I have interviewed hundreds of families that described their loved one as suffering from "hardening of the arteries," "little strokes," "dementia," "organic brain syndrome," or just old age and forgetfulness. A correct diagnosis is important, even if there is no treatment for the condition. The diagnosis is important so that other treatable conditions can be ruled out and the family can plan ahead for the problems that occur with Alzheimer's disease. Professionals in the field of aging usually refer to Alzheimer's disease as Senile Dementia of the Alzheimer's type (SDAT). Dementia is a word that describes clinical syndromes which are characterized by memory loss, poor judgment, behavioral changes, impaired learning, and difficulty managing self-care activities. There are different diseases that cause dementia in the elderly. The disease-causing dementia on which we will focus in this chapter is Alzheimer's disease.

Cause and Diagnosis

ALZHEIMER'S IS A DISEASE OF THE BRAIN. Briefly described, the cells of the brain are destroyed or altered. Brain physiology is very complicated, and a complete account of the brain changes in Alzheimer's disease is beyond the scope of this book. All that the caregiver needs to know is that the brain cells and the chemical activity in the brain are affected with this disease, and it is these brain changes that cause the problems associated with Alzheimer's disease. Although nobody really knows what causes this disease, several theories have been postulated. Some researchers believe that the disease is caused by a slow-acting virus. The disease is not contagious, so there is no need for the caregiver to worry. Some believe the disease is caused by malfunctions in the immune system or by accumulation in the brain of toxic substances from the environment. There may also be a genetic cause of the disease in some cases; however the fact that your parent has the disease doesn't necessarily mean that you will get it. Some scientists believe that the disease is caused by a number of factors and not just one of those mentioned in the theories above. Whatever the cause may be, unfortunately, there have been no successful treatments or cures to reverse or stop the progression of this illness.

The diagnosis of Alzheimer's disease is usually made by doing a complete physical examination and conducting a thorough evaluation of patient and family history. There is no specific test for the disease, but there are tests that can be used to rule out other reversible causes of memory loss. If you suspect that your loved one is suffering from dementia, have a thorough evaluation done by a competent physician. If the family physician is not comfortable doing an evaluation, ask for a referral to a neurologist or psychiatrist who is trained in dementia evaluation.

One of the things you can do as a caregiver is to recognize reversible causes of memory problems and behavioral changes in your parent. Alzheimer's disease is a progressive illness that usually gets worse over months or years. If your loved one, in a very short period of time, experiences changes in mental function, there may be an acute problem. Usually over-medication or improper use of medication causes an acute change in mental function. This problem should be evaluated by the physician immediately.

Other problems causing acute changes in mental function include infections, chemical imbalance in the blood, head injury due to falls, stroke, dehydration, and even shock. The physician can rule out reversible causes of dementia by doing blood work and other diagnostic tests. Scans of the brain may also be utilized to diagnose dementia, but these scans don't conclusively diagnose Alzheimer's disease. The scan may indicate atrophy (shrinkage of tissue) in the brain, but this in itself is not an indication of Alzheimer's disease. The brain scans are used primarily to locate any tumors or lesions in the brain that may cause symptoms similar to those of Alzheimer's disease. The only accurate way to diagnose Alzheimer's disease is after death, by doing an autopsy and studying the changes in the brain tissue.

Symptoms of the disease may be almost unnoticeable at first and may develop slowly, over time. The person with the disease may be the first to notice difficulty with concentration or carrying out daily chores. Complaints of memory loss or poor concentration by the patient may not necessarily indicate Alzheimer's disease, however. Many of the patients forget that they can't remember, and they may not even complain about memory problems. Memory complaints, along with poor motivation, behavioral problems and other similar characteristics of early Alzheimer's disease, may stem from depression and may be misdiagnosed as Alzheimer's disease. Depression is also common in the Alzheimer's patient and proper treatment may improve function. For further information on depression, you may want to review Chapter 5.

For Alzheimer's sufferers with whom I work, the disease tends to progress at different rates. The disease may have similar symptoms, yet the symptoms may show up differently, with varying severity, among different patients. I have generally found that no two people with Alzheimer's disease are the same.

When the disease begins to surface, simple things such as remembering names and appointments may cause concern. Difficulty with simple arithmetic can cause errors in writing checks or balancing the checkbook. If your loved one still works, problems in work performance may develop. Problems with initiating, following through, and completing tasks may also be evident. Your loved one may know she needs to make tea and not remember how to put water in the pot or turn on the stove. Once the water is boiled, she may forget to remove the kettle from the stove or turn off the burner. If these things happen occasionally, there is probably no need for concern. If these things happen consistently and memory problems seem to be getting worse, you should consult a physician.

People with Alzheimer's disease may have difficulty with the most simple of daily activities. Learning new tasks is very difficult, and the ability to retain information is impaired. The brain controls our memory, thoughts, judgment, intelligence, mood, feelings, personality, and ability to manage our environment. All these areas of life are affected in the Alzheimer's patient. As the disease progresses, the patient may become more dependent upon others to survive. Judgment may be impaired so that safety becomes a problem. The ability to eat, bathe, walk, go to the bathroom, and recognize familiar people and objects may become significantly impaired in time. Problems in behavior such as aggressiveness, poor control of impulses, wandering, agitation, repetitive motion or questions, yelling out, and suspiciousness may cause a great deal of stress to the patient and the family. It is these behaviors, along with difficulties in managing the physical care of an Alzheimer's patient, that lead to nursing home placement.

There is a reason why we call Alzheimer's disease a family affliction. The behaviors, challenges and care needs of an Alzheimer's victim place a tremendous responsibility on the family. Often the family is not prepared to handle the burden, and caregivers suffer tremendous stress, guilt and anxiety. You may have heard reports in the news about frustrated, stressed caregivers, who—with no hope left—have taken the life of the family member with Alzheimer's disease. This type of activity has been referred to in the press as mercy killing or euthanasia. Family caregivers and professionals who care for the elderly patient with terminal Alzheimer's disease may understand how these things can happen. Most other people however, including the legal scholars, find it difficult to understand how one can take the life of a terminally ill, demented individual. This chapter is meant to assist the caregiver in managing life with a family member suffering from Alzheimer's disease. Although there is no treatment for the disease, the caregiver's learning ways to cope can still be beneficial.

I have heard the cries and woes of caregivers many times; as I have listened, I've noticed that the questions always seem to begin with the word *why*. Why does she forget? Why does she ask the same question over and over again? Why doesn't she know night from day? Why does she get dressed and undressed over and over? Why does she ask to go home? Why does she accuse everyone of stealing from her? Why does she use foul language when she never cursed a day in her life before? Why does she forget everything I ask her to do? Why does she not recognize her family members as family? Why does she seem so normal sometimes, yet seem so confused at other times. Why does all this have to be happening to our family?

My response to caregivers is, "Why are you asking *why*?" You can search for answers to the question *why*, but the answer will usually be that the person is acting this way because of the disease process in the brain. Focusing on the *why* or placing blame on the victim will usually be fruitless.

Most behaviors exhibited by the Alzheimer's patient are beyond the patient's control. Don't blame your loved one, and try not to get angry. Also, don't blame yourself for not knowing or anticipating what the problem is. You can only do your best, and even your best may never be good enough. Instead of asking *why*, you should be asking *how*. How can I react to certain behaviors exhibited by my loved one with Alzheimer's, so that we obtain the desired results? How can I get her to remain in one place long enough to get dressed or eat? How can I react when she can't express herself? How can I take care of myself as a caregiver, so that I have the energy to care for my loved one who is afflicted by this terrible disease? How can I develop my patience so that things won't upset me so much as a caregiver?

The caregiver must be patient and understanding and have a tremendous amount of ingenuity. Most of the answers to caregiving problems will not be found in books. Nor will many answers be given to you by health professionals. You will learn by doing, guessing, trying, succeeding and sometimes failing. You can also learn how to care for the Alzheimer's patient from other caregivers. I recommend to all my patients' families that they join a support group for Alzheimer's caregivers. Not only do support groups provide fellowship and a place to share feelings, they may offer practical caregiving information and tips.

One of the most challenging aspects of caring for Alzheimer's patients is trying to figure out how they feel and what they are experiencing in their world. Imagine for a moment how your world would be if you didn't have a memory. How frustrating and scary it must be to wake up in the morning and find in your bed a stranger who says he is your husband, when you have no recollection of ever being married. How degrading it must be to feel the urge to use the toilet and wet yourself because you forgot where the bathroom was. How would it feel if, in your mind, you thought your home was the place in which you grew up, yet you couldn't get back there? This alone would be frightening, but if everyone was telling you that you were at home now, whom could you trust? I don't want to belabor the point, but it is important that the caregiver try to put herself in the head of the Alzheimer's victim and imagine the feeling.

When I respond to the Alzheimer's victim, I try to deal with feelings, rather than correcting information that is not accurate. If a patient is upset and crying that she wants to go home, telling her a hundred times that this is her home will not make her feel better. To her, she is not at home, and she will probably not be able to understand your explanation. Instead of arguing or correcting, I respond in a way that will deal with feelings, then try to redirect the person's attention to a pleasant thought.

As an example, if the person is crying to go home, perhaps she is scared or lonely. I may say to her, "I understand that you want to go home, and I'm sure that it's frightening to be here. You are safe right now, and we care very much for you. Your family also knows where you are, so there's no need to worry about them. Is there anything I can get you? Let's look around a little bit so you can feel comfortable being here."

By dealing with the feelings associated with the problem, you may be more successful. When this doesn't work, try to redirect the energy of the person; she may soon forget what she was originally upset about.

Just like the mother of an infant, the caregiver will grow to learn how to anticipate needs of a loved one. If a certain disturbing behavior is exhibited, keep track of what activity preceded the behavior and what interventions helped to resolve the problem. Keep the world around your loved one as simple and practical as possible, yet don't treat her like a baby and do everything for her. It is best to allow your loved one to do for herself as much as possible, so that she doesn't become excessively dependent and discouraged. At the same time, you should be aware of your loved one's limitations, so that safety is not compromised and frustration or failure with the activity doesn't lead to agitation, sadness and anger.

Look first toward basic human needs when responding to problem behaviors or frustrations. Basic human needs include the needs for touch, warmth, comfort (freedom from pain), security (freedom from fear), food, water, freedom to move, sleep, acceptance, and ability to have control over surroundings (e.g., go to the bathroom when the urge arises or have another person listen when one is trying to communicate). We all know what the needs of people are, and these needs are present no matter what our age or life situation. It is not that the needs of the Alzheimer's victim are so different. The problem is that the needs can't always be expressed in a way that others understand and respond to appropriately. Because there is such difficulty with communication and understanding in the Alzheimer's patient, you shouldn't always accept responses to questions at face value. You may ask if your loved one wishes to go to the bathroom, and she may not even remember what the word bathroom means. Getting angry will just add to her frustration and your guilt. If this is a problem, perhaps you can develop a toileting schedule so that accidents can be prevented. Maybe you can even show her a picture of a toilet and ask if she wants to go. She may relate to the picture, yet have no idea what the word bathroom means. Do what is practical; do what works for you and your loved one.

Again, let me emphasize the importance of remembering that no two people with Alzheimer's disease are alike; the caregiver needs to be creative in problem solving. If your loved one is restless and pacing, maybe you should take her for a long walk instead of medicating her. If she doesn't sleep at night—a common occurrence with Alzheimer's patients—perhaps you should eliminate daytime naps and assist her in exercise before giving a sleeping pill.

It is not uncommon for Alzheimer's patients to lose weight and not eat. If poor attention or concentration is a problem that interferes with eating, removing distractions such as television or conversation may be helpful. If noise and social engagement encourages eating, then by all means provide it. If utensils are difficult to use, prepare simple, nutritious, finger foods. If you can't get your loved one to sit still for any period of time, provide several small meals that can be eaten quickly. You can get nutritional supplements that offer a high number of calories in a limited volume of food or fluid. These supplements, such as Ensure® and Sustacal®, are available at your local drug store and can be good supplements. Remember that while water is still important, the disease may impair thirst or the ability to ask for water. Provide adequate fluids throughout the day.

Home safety is a very important issue with the memory impaired individual. Without understanding the consequences, a memory impaired person may drink dangerous chemicals, start a fire, discharge a loaded firearm, leave on the gas, wander away and get lost, drive away in the car and crash, take an overdose of medication, spill boiling water, step into a tub of water that is too hot, let a stranger into the house, give away money, or do any number of things that may be dangerous. Home safety is a must; I refer readers to Chapter 4.

Taking away privileges from a memory impaired family member is painful. A little pain initially, however, may save a lot of pain later on. You want to maximize independence and freedom, but you need not do so at the risk of compromising safety. In counseling caregivers of Alzheimer's patients, I recommend that they take certain steps to protect their loved ones. To keep the memory impaired person from getting lost and not being able to be identified, I suggest that an arm band be made up with the person's name, address, phone number, and words *memory impaired* engraved on the band. I would also keep recent pictures of your loved one on hand, in case she wanders away and needs to be identified by searchers. If your loved one wanders, you may need to install door locks that she can't negotiate. A locksmith can advise you on this. Be careful not to leave your loved one locked in the house alone, however, in case there is a fire and she needs to exit quickly. Also remember that locks can be a problem—especially locks on closets and bathrooms, where an elderly person may go in and not come out voluntarily. If you need to gain speedy access in an emergency, it may be difficult if the door you want to get into is locked. You may wish to remove these locks in the house.

Nobody really knows what causes a memory impaired person to wander. It may be that the disease restricts the person's ability to direct attention and energy. If you couldn't remember what you wanted to do, or if you started to do something and forgot what it was you were doing, maybe you, too, would wander aimlessly, trying to start or end something. Perhaps if you didn't know where you were, you might search for a place that was familiar and comfortable. Put yourself in the place of your memory impaired loved one, and try to imagine what she is going through. Whatever you do, don't try to argue with her when she is trying to wander away. Arguing may just add to her agitation, and you will have an agitated wanderer on your hands. Try to walk with her and redirect her, until she forgets what she is doing. If you can keep a record of when she wanders the most, perhaps you can determine what happens right before the wandering episode. If, for example, she wanders a half hour after lunch, perhaps she needs to go to the bathroom; assisting her to the bathroom after lunch may help. If she wanders a half-hour before lunch, perhaps she is hungry and looking for food. Giving the meal earlier may help the wandering. If she wanders when the sun goes down and light levels in the room decrease, perhaps turning on the lights before it gets dark will decrease the wandering behavior. When caring for the Alzheimer's patient, you need to be a very patient, loving detective.

I have assisted many adult children and spouses of people with Alzheimer's disease, and one of the most troublesome issues is dealing with problem behaviors. It is not uncommon for an Alzheimer's victim to accuse family members of stealing, abuse, imprisonment, or any number of uncomfortable things. Mom or Dad may have been a very timid, kind, and sensitive individual before the disease evolved. How does one react when kindness turns into anger? —politeness turns into rudeness? —passiveness turns into aggression? I instruct families to remember that the Alzheimer's victim usually can't help herself. Somehow these behaviors are easier to accept if you know that they are not intentional. People have difficulty understanding brain diseases and the resultant disabilities. After all, the person with Alzheimer's disease may look just fine on the outside but exhibit bizarre behaviors. If you met someone who was deaf, you wouldn't be upset if she couldn't hear you or respond appropriately to your questions. If you saw someone in a wheelchair who was paralyzed, you wouldn't expect that person to get up and walk with you. The person with Alzheimer's has a broken memory and an impaired brain. You cannot expect that person to respond to the surrounding environment as would someone with normal brain function.

This must be explained to children and other family members who have contact with the Alzheimer's victim. Young children are very sensitive about how adults treat them. If Grandma used to be loving to a grandchild and now accuses the grandchild of being an annoying neighbor kid who is stealing, the child may be devastated. It is important that you explain to the child that she hasn't done anything wrong and that Grandma still loves her. Explain that sometimes when people get older they get an illness that causes them to act the way Grandma is acting, but that Grandma still loves everyone. She just can't help the way she is acting. You need to emphasize to the child that this illness doesn't happen to everyone and it won't happen to the child or parent. You explain this, of course, at the child's level of understanding. You would explain this to a five-year-old differently than to a nine-year-old. Actually, children can be good medicine for an Alzheimer's victim, and supervised interaction is beneficial. I would be careful, however, about leaving a child with Grandmother as the baby-sitter, if the grandmother has a dementing illness.

When interacting with a loved one suffering from Alzheimer's disease, keep things as simple as possible. We learn and practice very simple tasks all our lives. Getting dressed, for example, seems so simple to us. We do it every day, and our biggest challenge is coordinating colors. Getting dressed when you have a memory impairment can be an all-day challenge. You may no longer remember what clothes are for. You may not remember that underwear goes on first. You may not know that pants go on the legs and shirts go on the torso. You may not remember how to button or zip a garment. You may not understand that you need to be dressed when you go out in public.

So imagine being memory impaired and having someone tell you to get dressed because you have a doctor's appointment in thirty minutes. Imagine how you would feel if the person got upset with you when you didn't get dressed on time. These struggles are daily events in the lives of caregivers and elderly victims of Alzheimer's disease.

When I say keep things simple, I mean *very* simple. You also must adjust difficult tasks according to the degree of impairment in your loved one. Keep in mind that once an ability is lost, there is a good possibility that it will not be regained by the Alzheimer's victim.

Take the simple example of getting your loved one dressed for an appointment. Neither leave her on her own, saying, "Get dressed, we are going," nor do it all yourself, putting each piece of clothing on her. Experiment to see what she can do for herself. Allow her to do as much as possible for herself, even if she makes mistakes. Don't scold or spend too much time trying to correct mistakes, and be sure to praise good results. Break the task down into many small goals. When assisting in dressing, explain simply that you are going to help your loved one get dressed. Don't ask her to choose what to wear from a closet full of clothes. Take out two appropriate outfits and give her a choice between the two. It is important to offer choices so that some autonomy is maintained. When one outfit is chosen, put the other one away.

Go into a quiet room with no distractions. Touch is very important when cuing a memory impaired person. Instead of saying "put your right hand through the sleeve," touch the hand that you wish put through the sleeve and assist in placing the arm so that the shirt goes on easily. Don't take for granted that your loved one remembers the right from the left hand. Touch and assist at the same time. If your loved one gets upset or fights your efforts to assist her, stop what you are doing and try again in a few minutes. It is very important to allow plenty of time when assisting an Alzheimer's victim, just in case you need to stop and start again later.

As the disease progresses, you may find that your loved one becomes more and more dependent upon you for even the most basic needs. You may need to assist with bathing, feeding, and even toileting your loved one. Different care needs create different amounts of stress and anguish in a caregiver. One caregiver may feel perfectly comfortable preparing meals and assisting with dressing, but when it comes to bathing or taking a parent to the toilet the caregiver can't handle it. Know what you are comfortable doing. If something makes you uncomfortable, see if you can get assistance in the home or try to figure out what the problem is. Support groups are available to help people caring for Alzheimer's victims. There is even an association called The Alzheimer's Disease and Related Disorders Association, which probably has local chapters in your area that would be willing to give information and help. Take advantage of whatever help is out there. If you try to do everything by yourself, your family may end up with two victims of this disease. Learn all you can by reading books on the subject and talking with people who share the same experience.

There are good and bad days when caring for your loved one with Alzheimer's disease. As a caregiver, you need to conserve your strength and energy and know when to ask for help. In Chapters 7 and 12, you will find valuable information on how to cope during rough times. If you don't bring help into the home, consider taking your parent or loved one to an adult day care center that admits Alzheimer's patients. Check with local senior centers or social service agencies in your area to find out if adult day care is available. Adult day care centers offer meals and activity during the day in a supervised environment. Many working adult children drop their parents off at such centers before work and pick them up after work. These centers can be very helpful if you are unable to leave a loved one alone during the day.

Many long term care nursing facilities are now opening up special Alzheimer's units that cater to the Alzheimer's patient and family. If the burden of caring for an Alzheimer's victim becomes too much on the caregiver, such facilities may be an alternative, assuming they are within one's financial means.

When choosing an Alzheimer's facility, be sure to ask what makes the facility you are looking at any different from a regular nursing home. Some facilities just put alarms on the doors and designate a certain area for Alzheimer's patients. This is by no means an Alzheimer's facility. A facility that claims to specialize in the care of Alzheimer's patients should have staff with special training, and you should ask what type of training is given. Activities should be offered that are geared toward dementia patients, and there should be plenty of activity staff available on a twenty-four hour basis. The facility should be safe and secure for people who wander; outdoor grounds are a plus. Ask about the facility architecture and features in the environment that make it specially geared for the Alzheimer's patient. Ask how they handle certain behaviors which your loved one may be exhibiting, and learn their philosophy on restraints and medications. Also ask what type of support is available for the caregiver.

Even if you are able to get help with the physical aspects of care, you may still have the emotional stress and anguish of dealing with the loss of your loved one. When I talk of loss, I don't mean physical loss. I mean the loss of the person whom you once knew. I have helped many adult children and spouses work through their feelings about caring for a family member with Alzheimer's. After a while, many caregivers feel that the situation is hopeless as they watch their loved one slip away. Feelings of hopelessness are common when people believe they have no control over what is happening around them. The main focus of caring for an elderly person with Alzheimer's disease is that the caregiver will eventually have to take control of the victim's future and well-being. Taking control may mean making difficult decisions for someone who can no longer understand what is going on around her. If you are informed and confident in what you are doing as a caregiver, then feelings of hopelessness are less likely to surface. My hope is that this chapter on Alzheimer's disease and other chapters in this book improve your knowledge base and help you gain control over a difficult challenge. For further information and support on Alzheimer's disease, you may contact the national headquarters of the Alzheimer's Association by calling 1-800-621-0379 (in Illinois, call 1-800-572-6037) or writing to Alzheimer's Association, 919 N. Michigan Avenue, Suite 1000, Chicago IL 60611-1676.

It is important to mention another potential cause of mental impairment in the elderly; it is termed vascular, or multi-infarct, dementia. Multi-infarct dementia is caused by diseases in the blood vessels that supply blood to the brain. When blood supply to the brain is disturbed, the result may be mini-strokes, which may cause damage to the brain. This brain damage, in turn, can cause symptoms of dementia (mental impairment). Multi-infarct dementia can be diagnosed by the physician; the way the disease presents itself, as well as potential treatment for it, may be different from Alzheimer's disease. You should keep in mind, however, that people with Alzheimer's disease may also suffer from vascular or multi-infarct. Symptoms of multi-infarct dementia may appear suddenly, and deterioration in function may be in steps—as opposed to the grandual onset and progression of Alzheimer's disease. Your loved one's physician will be able to perform tests to determine if the memory loss or decline in mental function is due to multi-infarct dementia. If it is, the problem may be treatable; appropriate medical intervention may prevent or delay the devastation of a potential stroke in the future.

16

WHEN DRIVING BECOMES UNSAFE

Some of my fondest memories have begun with a car trip with my husband, Sam. Now, even a short trip is terrifying. Lately, as the cupboards in the house need restocking, I get a nervous feeling in my stomach because I know that it means a trip with Sam in the car. On Sam's eighty-first birthday, two years ago, he barely passed the driving test because of his poor vision, but his bad memory wasn't even a consideration. The gentleman testing Sam didn't know about his difficulty with remembering; since the man gave Sam specific directions on what to do, he passed. Two years have gone by, and Sam has been diagnosed with Alzheimer's disease. His memory is getting worse, and he gets lost and impatient even on our short trips.

We've been married more than fifty years, and I regret that I never learned how to drive a car. I never had the need to drive, because Sam was always there to take me around. If Sam wasn't around to drive me, I would walk. Can you imagine that? Where we used to live, everything was in walking distance, and it was safe to walk the streets alone at night. These days Sam and I both have difficulty walking, but even if we could walk, the grocery store is too far away.

Something as simple as driving to the grocery store causes so much stress in our life. Sam doesn't want to admit that he has difficulty driving, and he argues when I bring it up. He has always taken so much pride in his car and in driving me around. I can remember when he picked me up for our first date. He was so proud of his old Ford truck. It barely ran. As a matter of fact, if my memory serves me, the old Ford broke down on that first date and we had to walk a few miles to get home. Those were the days.

Maybe if I call our daughter, she can reason with Sam. He loves to see her. Maybe she could pick up some groceries for us each week or take us shopping. I don't want to be a burden, but I'm frightened that Sam might hurt us or, even worse, injure an innocent person if he keeps driving. I'll pray on it tonight. God has been so good to us that I'm sure He will help me find an answer to this problem.

As you can see from this story, something as simple to a younger adult as driving, can create extreme stress for our elderly parents. It is also common for our elderly parents not to discuss the issue of driving privileges for fear of losing independence or being a burden. The focus of this chapter is to help the adult child at least recognize the issue of safe driving and deal with the challenge appropriately.

Remember what you wanted most when you were about 15 years old? If you were a normal teenager, I'll bet you begged your parents for a car. A car meant independence. You didn't have to rely on your mom, dad or big brother or sister to take you anywhere. Driving was a milestone that meant maturity. If you are like most people, your mom or dad probably gave you your first driving lesson and decided when you were ready to get your driver's license. As an adult child of an aging parent, you may find it difficult to recommend to Mom and Dad that they no longer drive. The safety of elderly parents and others on the road should be of utmost concern. The biggest question most caregivers have is how to determine when driving is no longer safe. The second question is how to take the privilege away without damaging their parents' self-esteem or independent functioning. As with many other topics discussed in caring for your aging parent, prevention is of utmost importance.

YOU DON'T WANT TO WAIT FOR A SERIOUS OR FATAL ACCIDENT BEFORE THIS ISSUE IS ADDRESSED!

A good number of people can safely drive in their later years, but the caregiver should be aware of some common conditions that contribute to possible risks. The most obvious impediment to safe driving is impaired vision. Many elderly people see poorly at night and even avoid night driving altogether. During the day, glare may pose a problem, especially if the elderly person has cataracts. Decreases in peripheral vision may limit the ability to see cross traffic. Decreased visual acuity may cause difficulty seeing street signs. Whether loss of hearing affects driving safety depends on the amount of hearing loss and the ability of the elderly driver to compensate with good eyesight.

Neurological impairments due to Alzheimer's disease, Parkinson's Disease, or strokes may affect an elderly driver's judgment, reaction time, and/or ability to maneuver an automobile. Elderly people with memory impairments may not know what to do at a stop sign, may go at a red light and stop at a green light, or may drive and drive without knowing how to get where they are going or how to get home.

In addition to the physiological and medical conditions that may make driving unsafe for your elderly loved one, medications may contribute to impaired driving ability. Many elderly people take tranquilizers, pain medicines, sleep medicines, anti-anxiety medicine, or other medicines that may cause a decreased level of consciousness. You need to be aware that driving is a hazard for your elderly parent if these medicines are being taken. Remember also that the effect of these medications may be minimal to a young healthy adult but be devastating to a frail, elderly person. Alcohol is also a potent drug; when combined with central nervous system depressant medications, it can be deadly. Drunk driving is not just limited to teenagers and young adults. The elderly are also at risk. Be aware and take precautions.

Laws regarding impaired drivers vary from state to state. In some states physicians are required to report impaired elderly drivers to the motor vehicle department. The motor vehicle department will in turn give the driver a written and driving test to determine the ability to drive safely. In some states, after a certain age the license will not be renewed without a vision and driving test.

Whether to withdraw driving privileges from an elderly loved one is a difficult judgment call. It should be a group decision, with involvement of family, elderly driver, physician and local motor vehicle authority. It may not be necessary to completely take away driving privileges if a driver is impaired. Privileges may be curtailed to daytime driving, driving a limited distance, or driving with a friend in the car for assistance. A driver's license is not automatically revoked just because an elderly person is reported as a possible driving risk. In California the law requires a physician to report to the authorities any patient, elderly or otherwise, who may have lapses of consciousness or functional disabilities that make driving unsafe. Failure of a physician to report such conditions may make the physician liable, should an accident result from an unreported condition. Be aware that if you get the physician involved in the decision to remove driving privileges, he may have no choice but to report your elderly loved one.

You should approach this subject by going for a drive with your elderly parent to get a feel for how things are. Be sure that both of you are strapped in. Make observations about your parent's driving too slow or too fast, stopping suddenly, safely changing lanes, ability to see and interpret street signs, reaction time, and frustration and anxiety while driving.

Ask your elderly parent how she feels about driving. Is driving perceived as a burden or as a key to independence? If you are concerned about your loved one's driving ability, the issue should be openly discussed. The physician may be a good facilitator for the discussion, as well as a good resource to evaluate functional and mental abilities to still drive. The physician may also be able to recommend interventions that may assist driving by improving vision, changing medications, or using assistive devices. If your loved one has Alzheimer's disease or another neurological illness that affects memory, it may be difficult for her to have enough insight to understand why you need to remove the driving privilege. Be sure that when you have a discussion about removing driving privileges that you do so with your elderly parent's dignity in mind. Try not to argue. You may say that many people voluntarily give up driving to protect innocent people from getting hurt in an accident. You can emphasize to Mom and Dad that they would feel awful if they had an accident and hurt a little child. By giving up driving now, they can avoid the emotional trauma of an accident to themselves and another family. You may also bring into the discussion the unnecessary cost of keeping up a car and automobile insurance if they don't drive too much. If explanations fail with someone who has memory impairment, you may need to remove the car keys or disable the car by removing the battery or distributor cap. You may even be better off to remove the car, so that the reminder to drive is no longer there.

Keep in mind that the intent is not always to remove driving privileges. Do what you can to enable your elderly parent to drive as long as it is safe. When driving is no longer safe and the privilege is taken away, some form of transportation must be available. Without a substitute for the car, your elderly loved one may feel anxious, depressed or isolated. Public transportation may be a possibility, but it is difficult for an elderly individual who is *not* impaired to negotiate the public transportation system. Getting on and off a bus and sitting down with a walker is quite difficult. It is also difficult to figure out routes and schedules. Some areas have special transportation for the elderly, so that they can be picked up and dropped off at the door. These buses are equipped to accommodate the elderly, and drivers are trained to assist an elderly person. Check with your local hospital discharge planner or senior center to find out about the availability of such services. Of course, many retirement centers provide transportation and outings and even help with socialization. You don't want to move Mom or Dad to a retirement center just because they can no longer drive, but be aware that this is one advantage to congregate living.

For medical appointments, check with local physician and hospital groups. We are increasingly seeing competing medical groups providing transportation to the elderly to and from the office, as competition for business increases. You may also try to arrange for your parent's doctor to make a house call, or you may find a doctor who still will do so. Doctors can gather valuable information on your parent's functional abilities and living environment by coming to the house. If shopping is a problem, you may arrange a couple of days a week for a family member, friend or hired helper to take your parent shopping. Bringing your elderly parent along when you shop for your family may be a good time for interaction. Some grocery stores still deliver, and "Meals on Wheels" may be delivered to the home if your parent qualifies. You can check with your local Area Agency on Aging for available in-home services. Look in the phone book for the number, or call your state agency on aging, listed in the Resource Guide at the end of this book.

As you are finding by reading this book and from personal experience, decisions a caregiver must make are not always easy. Taking away the privilege to drive may be a difficult, but life saving, decision. Be honest, kind and compassionate, but remain firm if you believe that continued driving by your elderly parent may be a safety hazard. Be creative; try to get some of your parents' neighbors involved. This is especially helpful if your parents live in an area with other elderly people. Perhaps another elderly person in the neighborhood can still drive but doesn't do much cooking. Ask your elderly parent about neighbors and empower them to get together. The neighbor can do the driving and your parent and the neighbor can shop together. Perhaps the neighbor doing the driving can no longer do the cooking. In exchange for the drive to the market, your parent can cook the neighbor a few meals. When you try to help with any issue, you should ask for your parent's ideas and try not to intervene in a way that causes feelings of helplessness. If your parent can no longer drive, there may be something she can do in return for the favor of another's driving, so that she can still maintain her dignity and self-worth.

If you gain nothing else from reading this chapter, I hope you have become aware, as an adult child of an aging parent, that driving may be a concern even if it is not brought up by your parent. Go for a drive with your parent every so often to observe her driving skills. Perhaps you can intervene before a major problem arises.

17

UNDERSTANDING AND COPING WITH INCONTINENCE

THERE ARE PROBABLY VERY FEW THINGS that are more uncomfortable to talk about with our elderly parents than incontinence. Simply defined, incontinence is the involuntary loss of urine or feces. Many elderly people remain silent about their suffering from incontinence, for fear of embarrassment or institutionalization. Many others simply live with the condition, thinking that it is just a normal development as one ages. Incontinence is not a normal condition of aging, nor is it something our elderly loved ones should just accept and live with. If your elderly parent suffers from incontinence, a proper evaluation should be undertaken, and appropriate management should be initiated.

From a very young age our parents taught us how to control our bowels and bladders. They expended money and time, buying and/or laundering diapers and trying to toilet train us, until we successfully completed the task. When we wet the bed or soiled our clothing, they may have embarrassed or punished us. After all, big boys and girls didn't use diapers. Try to imagine for a moment being an elderly adult who can no longer control such a basic bodily function as urination. Many such elderly people are afraid to leave the house or participate in any social activity, for fear of having an "accident." This social isolation and fear can lead to depression and even further decline in function. As caregivers of our elderly parents, we have a duty and responsibility to investigate the problem of incontinence and to assist in its evaluation and management.

Incontinence has multiple causes and varying degrees of severity. The purpose of this section is to educate caregivers on the general principles of urinary tract dysfunction in the elderly. With this information, the caregiver should at least be able to recognize the problem and have a basic idea of what kind of assistance is available. Even if the incontinence cannot be cured, the caregiver who is well informed may be of tremendous assistance in management of the problem. The following scenario is played out by caregivers and elderly people daily. My hope and prayer is that after reading this information you can deal with it effectively or, perhaps, even avoid what this family is going through.

Mom used to look forward to our visits, especially when I brought her grandson Josh with me. Not long ago, Mom stopped being enthusiastic when I'd tell her we were coming to see her. We used to be able to just drop by, but she started insisting that I call first. When I called, she'd only want us to come at certain times of the day. She said she just wasn't up to taking visitors.

About three weeks ago when we visited the retirement hotel, I noticed that Mom's apartment had a faint smell of urine. She was used to having me go to the closet to take the laundry home to wash, but that day she got angry and told me that she had no clothes that needed washing. She actually took my arm and led me away from the closet. I knew something was wrong, because I could see the hamper almost overflowing. Mom looked very tired. When I asked her how she was sleeping, she mentioned that she had been having to get up several times in the night to go to the bathroom. She seemed unusually anxious and wanted us to leave.

Driving home, I actually got annoyed with Mom for not appreciating our visit. I wondered if I had done something to make her angry. As silly as it sounds, I decided not to visit again until she called and asked me to come see her. Maybe then she wouldn't treat us like strangers. Well, a week passed and there was no call from Mom. After the second week with no call, I began to feel uneasy. I was concerned for good reason, because three weeks after our visit I got a phone call from the administrator at the retirement hotel where Mom lives. She said that because Mom hadn't come down for meals in awhile, they'd visited her in her apartment to see what was wrong. When they entered the apartment, it smelled terribly of urine, and they found Mom to be incontinent.

I didn't even know what the word incontinent meant until I got that phone call, and now they are telling me that we have to move Mom to a nursing home because they don't allow incontinent residents. If we don't move her to a nursing home, they want us to hire a private aide to make sure that she gets the care that she needs. I should have seen it coming weeks ago, or even a couple of months ago, when Mom started acting strange. Mom will not go to a nursing home, and I know she won't allow anyone to stay with her. I can't take her home with me. What in the world am I going to do? They can't just kick her out of her apartment because of this incontinence thing, can they? Somebody must know what we can do to get help.

The scenario above is not at all uncommon. The somebody who will know how to help is the informed caregiver. That somebody is you.

Incontinence is quite common in the elderly and has a wide variety of causes. In many cases the problem is reversible, while for some others the problem is at least manageable with appropriate intervention. In order to understand the causes and treatment of incontinence, it is important to know a little bit about normal function of the bladder.

Several functions in the body have to work in harmony for normal urination to take place. The bladder must be capable of storing urine, and the body must be able to recognize when the bladder is full and should be emptied. If the urinary anatomical outlet is obstructed or unable to be voluntarily controlled, then urinary incontinence may occur. Proper urination requires complex signals from the brain and nervous system that go beyond the scope of explanation in this section. From a neurological perspective, it is sufficient for you to know that your elderly parent has to have good enough memory and neurological function to know that she has to use the toilet at the proper time. She also needs to remember how to find the toilet when she feels the need to urinate. If she needs to urinate in a hurry, she has to have the ability to walk to the bathroom, get undressed and get on the toilet before she loses control.

As caregivers for our elderly parent, we must keep in mind that incontinence is not a normal result of the aging process. In many cases incontinence is caused by a reversible process that can be evaluated and treated. Keep in mind that the physiology of an elderly person is very delicate, and incontinence may be an indication of an impending acute illness. Like falls and delirium (discussed in Chapter 4), incontinence may be a result of an imbalance in the elderly person's physiology. If incontinence develops suddenly, you should be sure to have your parent evaluated promptly by a physician. Something as simple as a urinary tract infection can be a treatable cause of incontinence.

The other association between incontinence and acute illness in the elderly has to do with immobility. If your elderly parent is weak, staying in bed, and having worsening heart failure, incontinence may occur as a result of not being able to get to the toilet when necessary. Uncontrolled, chronic medical conditions such as diabetes may also worsen and cause temporary urinary incontinence; thus it is important that any such chronic illness is properly managed. Keep in mind that in the elderly, who have delicate physiology and decreased reserves for recovery, any minor change in condition may start a downward spiral of events that can contribute to the development of incontinence.

Perhaps the most common and significant cause of transient, reversible incontinence is problems with medications. Many elderly people take several medications at one time. Some medications, alone or in combination, can contribute to incontinence. If your elderly parent experiences trouble with incontinence, it would be wise to investigate all over-the-counter and prescription drugs as possible causes. Make a list of the medications—or gather them up—and have them evaluated by the doctor or pharmacist. Also be aware that having the instructions written on the bottle doesn't mean that your parent is taking the medication properly. (See Chapter 6.)

Some medications that can lead to urinary incontinence include diuretics, antidepressants, sleep medications, anti-anxiety medicines, and high blood pressure medicines. Each class of drugs has a specific action that can possibly lead to incontinence; adjusting the medication's dosage or timing may help reverse the condition. Consider, for example, an elderly parent who takes a diuretic (water pill) too often or before bedtime. The diuretic may cause excessive urination during the night, leading to an inability to control urine. A sleep medication may cause an abnormally deep sleep, so that the need to urinate is not recognized. A wet bed may be the result. If acute incontinence develops, check to see if a medication was just started, stopped or changed, and get a thorough evaluation by a physician.

After an acute illness or medication problem has been ruled out as the cause of incontinence, it is time to investigate more chronic causes of involuntary loss of urine in the elderly. An evaluation by a urologist (a physician who deals with urinary tract problems) is indicated if your elderly parent is experiencing incontinence. I would recommend that you ask for a referral to a physician who has experience in evaluating incontinent, elderly patients. Family doctors may have little training in the causes and treatments of incontinence in the elderly, so push for the referral. If your elderly parent's doctor tells you that it is just old age, then perhaps it is time to find a new doctor. Do not give up until you get a complete evaluation describing possible causes of the problem and treatment options.

Because incontinence is such a complex subject, a thorough discussion is beyond the scope of this book. A general idea of possible causes and treatments may, however, help you to be a more informed health care consumer. An idea of different types of incontinence will help you and your elderly parent understand what is happening.

To facilitate the evaluation by a physician, you can assist your elderly parent in monitoring and describing symptoms. Such monitoring can sometimes lead to discovering the cause of the problem. Keep track, or have your elderly parent keep track, of how often she needs to urinate and what the feeling is prior to needing to urinate. (For example: "All of a sudden, I have to urinate, and I can't make it to the bathroom on time," or, "I cough and urine leaks out," or, "I try to urinate and nothing comes out," or, "My bladder feels full," or, "My bladder feels like it is forcefully contracting," or, "It burns when I urinate.") Have your parent describe the feeling in her own words. If possible, keep track of the time of day urination occurs, as well as how much urine is voided. Ask your parent's doctor for assistance in monitoring the problem. The treatment of incontinence often requires active participation of the doctor, patient and family.

Some causes of chronic incontinence may include:
- a hyperactive bladder that contracts abnormally and causes uncontrolled urination;
- a bladder that inadequately empties, leaving it with leftover urine that leaks out;
- weakness in muscles that control the opening and closing of the urinary tract, so that urine may leak when one coughs, laughs or sneezes;
- a bladder that retains urine because of an obstruction in the urinary tract, causing it to become overfilled and leak;
- deterioration in memory due to brain and nervous system disorders, leading to incontinence;
- environmental barriers to getting to the toilet, undressed and on the commode (treatable with assistance in the home).

Management of incontinence in your elderly parent can include treatment with medication; surgery to correct physical abnormalities; and behavior therapy, such as biofeedback and exercises, to increase and control urinary tract muscle tone and control. The use of adult diapers and pads is not in itself a treatment for incontinene, and I urge families to get a thorough evaluation of an elderly parent prior to using diapers. The use of diapers can be beneficial, but keep in mind that the use of diapers without a good reason can lead to increased dependence and regression.

In summary, incontinence in an elderly parent is not a

hopeless condition. As caregivers we need to openly discuss and actively assist our parent in the evaluation and treatment of this potentially devastating problem. If you suspect an incontinence problem with your elderly parent, don't wait for things to get better on their own. Get professional help and offer your support.

18

COMMON INFECTIONS

URINARY TRACT INFECTION, LUNG INFECTION (PNEUMONIA)

INFECTIONS ARE COMMON TO ALL AGE GROUPS, but the elderly may have increased susceptibility to infections due to chronic diseases, alterations in lifestyle and nutrition, decreases in immune function, and changes in physiology that accompany aging. Infections may also have more serious consequences, especially in the very frail elderly, who have limited ability to recover. Because of the serious problems and functional declines that can be associated with infections, it is important for the caregiver to be able to recognize the early signs of infections and seek medical assistance for elderly loved ones as soon as possible. It is beyond the scope of this book to describe the causes and treatments of every infection, so the focus will be on the two most common sites of infection in the elderly: the urinary tract and the lungs.

Urinary tract infections are very common in the elderly; if not recognized and treated promptly in the very old, they can lead to septicemia (infection throughout the body) or death. Many factors lead to the increased infection rate and recurrent infections in the elderly. Among these factors are:

- Elderly people may have decreased immune system responses, so they cannot mount an adequate response to fight infections.

- Changes in the anatomy of the urinary system may allow bacteria to attack and invade the urinary system.

- As one ages, the bladder may not completely empty upon urination, and the residual urine may provide a good medium in which the bacteria can grow.

- Older people may have catheters (tubes in the urethra and bladder to allow the emptying of urine); any foreign object in the body can introduce bacteria and allow them to grow.

- Poor hygiene and fecal incontinence (inability to control bowel movements) may contaminate the urinary tract and contribute to urinary tract infections; bacteria from the colon, primarily Escherichia Coli, may invade the bladder.

Symptoms of a urinary tract infection may include an urgent desire to urinate, burning or pain when urinating, and a frequent need to urinate. Any of these symptoms reported by your elderly loved one should be evaluated by a physician. Sometimes the symptoms may not be reported, especially if she has memory impairment or difficulty communicating. If your loved one is incontinent, the symptoms of a urinary infection may be attributed to incontinence and just ignored. For these reasons, it is important to be vigilant as a caregiver; watch and ask about signs and symptoms of a urinary tract infection.

If an infection is suspected, the physician will probably take a urine sample and prescribe antibiotics. Be sure to give the antibiotics as prescribed and finish the prescription, unless advised otherwise. It is very important to follow up with the physician until the infection is resolved. Remember that adequate fluid intake is important, too. In addition, you should ask the pharmacist and physician about possible side effects from the antibiotics.

In some cases the physician may find bacteria in your loved one's urine but decide not to prescribe antibiotics unless symptoms of infection are present. Antibiotics must be prudently prescribed to prevent resistance of the bacteria to the antibiotics' effects. This precaution may be taken in case, at a later date, a more difficult infection must be treated and resolved. Discuss causes of the infection and treatment options with your elderly loved one's physician.

Keep in mind that an elderly person may not show symptoms in a typical fashion; the illness may develop rapidly and progress quickly into a major medical crisis. As a caregiver, you should try to recognize serious impending problems early, so that you can get rapid treatment for your loved one. If urinary tract infections are not recognized and treated early, the result may be urosepsis. When urosepsis develops, the infection in the bladder spreads throughout the bloodstream and causes major illness. Since symptoms in the elderly may differ from those of the young, urosepsis may show up in atypical ways. Your elderly loved one may stop eating, experience fever and chills, have falls, become lethargic and not herself, become disoriented when not normally disoriented, or if already disoriented become suddenly worse. Alertness to symptoms and prompt and appropriate treatment will help to avoid unnecessary hospital days, nursing home confinement, and declines in functional ability. With any illness in a frail, elderly person, confinement to bed or decreased mobility—even for a limited amount of time—can trigger excessive dependence and decreases in the independent ability to perform self-care activities.

Pneumonia (infection in the lungs) is another very common and serious infection in the elderly; it can lead to death and severe disability if not recognized and treated early. Even with prompt and adequate treatment, pneumonia is still one of the major causes of death in the elderly. As with urinary infections, changes with age make the elderly more susceptible to lung infections. The ability of the body to fight infection may decrease as one ages.

Elderly people may have difficulty swallowing and clearing secretions, so that bacteria normally found in the back of the throat may be exposed to the lungs. Older people may spend more time in hospitals and nursing homes, where there is an increased chance of acquiring infections. Older people may have a decreased ability to cough, so that bacteria are not expelled with mucous; and they may spend excessive amounts of time in bed, so that lungs get less activity and bacteria are not expelled through normal respiration.

The symptoms of pneumonia in the elderly may be different than that of the young. Typically a younger person with pneumonia may have a cough with sputum (mucous), as well as fever. Older people may have a lower baseline temperature and a decreased ability to mount an attack against infection with fever. The use of medications such as aspirin and Tylenol for pain in the elderly may also mask the sign of fever if an infection is present. For these reasons, a serious infection may not be accompanied by a fever. So don't wait for a high fever before you bring your loved one to the doctor. Nor should you wait for a serious cough with sputum to develop, since pneumonia in the elderly may not come with a cough.

If your elderly loved one suffers from chronic bronchitis or chronic obstructive pulmonary disease, then coughing may be a normal, everyday occurrence and not be recognized as a sign of impending pneumonia. Pneumonia in your elderly loved one may be suspected if she just doesn't seem herself, has a decreased appetite, is weak or lethargic, becomes disoriented, begins to fall or actually experiences cough and fever. If any such symptoms are experienced by your loved one, seek medical advice right away.

Treatment may include antibiotics, intravenous fluids and hospitalization. Unless the physician advised otherwise, be sure that adequate fluid intake is maintained, especially if there is fever present and if your loved one has a decreased appetite due to her illness. Ask your loved one's physician about preventive vaccination for influenza before the flu season, and be sure to assist your loved one in obtaining a vaccination if the physician so advises.

Early recognition and prompt treatment of infections is of utmost importance when caring for your elderly loved one. As a caregiver, your ability to notice signs and symptoms of urinary tract infections and pneumonia early may prevent increased disability in your elderly loved one; this would help you reduce the potential burden of care that may have developed had you not been well informed.

19

UNDERSTANDING DEHYDRATION AND MALNUTRITION

D EHYDRATION IS ONE SERIOUS PROBLEM for the elderly over which we, as caregivers, can exert control. Water and the chemicals in water, such as sodium and potassium, are the basis of human life. The physiology of the elderly may change, thus causing disturbances in the body's ability to regulate water and salt balance. Be sure that your elderly loved one drinks a sufficient amount of fluid, unless the doctor has her on fluid restrictions for some medical reason.

Older people may be susceptible to dehydration for many reasons. They may have a decreased thirst sensation. They may be afraid to drink water if they are incontinent and fear wetting themselves. Older people with memory loss may forget how to get water or not know what to do when they are thirsty. Medications may affect water balance and salts in the body. Diuretics ("water pills") are commonly prescribed for the elderly and may lead to dehydration or chemical imbalance in the blood, if not taken properly or with potassium supplementation.

Be alert to signs and symptoms of dehydration and excessive or deficient levels of potassium and/or sodium in the blood. Simple signs to look for include dry mucous membranes, fatigue, lethargy, dizziness, fainting, rapid pulse, confusion and disorientation when not normally present, or increased disorientation and confusion in someone already memory impaired. Another sympton of dehydration is poor skin elasticity. You can test your elderly loved one's skin turgor by lifting the skin on the forehead or arm and seeing how fast it snaps back. The skin's staying up or returning slowly may be a sign of dehydration.

The condition may have many causes, so be watchful for its development in your elderly loved one. If she has diarrhea or vomiting from the flu, dehydration can develop rapidly if fluids are not adequately replaced. A febrile illness in your elderly loved one may also lead to dehydration. If you suspect dehydration is developing in your loved one, seek the assistance of her physician right away. It may not be sufficient to just give oral fluids at home. Blood samples may be necessary, and intravenous fluids with proper mixtures of electrolytes may be life saving.

Malnutrition in our elderly parents and loved ones may result from several underlying factors, acting alone or in combination. Malnutrition may result from your loved one's consuming inadequate calories, consuming calories that are not balanced nutritionally, or lack of vitamins and minerals. Another cause may be disease states that prevent the body from properly assimilating the nutrients consumed, even if those nutrients are adequate for the normal person.

It is very important to discuss your elderly parent's nutritional status with her physician, especially if changes in appetite and weight have occurred. You may even want to suggest that the physician do blood studies on your elderly parent to measure the amount of serum protein (albumin), hemoglobin, iron, folate, calcium, zinc, vitamin B12, and thyroid levels in the blood. A thorough medical evaluation should be undertaken because of the relationship between weight loss and/or poor appetite and diseases in the elderly. If the underlying disease that is causing the weight loss and poor appetite can be identified and treated, then the state of nutrition may possibly be corrected with proper medical intervention.

Most of us are aware of the relationship between our moods and appetite. Some people eat excessively if they feel depressed or anxious. Others get an upset stomach or lose their appetite when feeling anxious or depressed. If weight loss and poor appetite occur along with signs and symptoms of depression, it is important to correct the underlying depression if proper nutrition is to be maintained. (See Chapter 5.)

Other factors that affect nutrition in the elderly may include the ability to see, smell, taste, chew, swallow, digest, assimilate and eliminate foods. The appearance of a nicely prepared or favorite food may stimulate appetite and make one's mouth water. Your elderly parent's appetite may not be as hearty as in the past, simply because she cannot see the food that she is preparing or eating. Correcting vision and lighting may aid in appetite stimulation. Decreases of taste and smell may normally accompany aging or may be caused by vitamin deficiencies, disease states or medications. Evaluate your elderly parent's ability to smell and taste food, if she has a poor appetite or doesn't enjoy eating. If her sense of taste or smell is inhibited, seek the advice of her physician. If he doesn't have an acceptable answer, ask for an appropriate specialist referral.

The inability to comfortably chew food may have a tremendous effect upon the nutritional status of your elderly parent. Painful gums and teeth, dry mouth, and dentures that no longer fit can all contribute to decreased intake of food. Proper dental care is just as important for the elderly as it is for our children. Even if your elderly parent is without teeth, regular examinations by a dentist are essential to identify and treat early states of oral diseases and cancer. If difficulty chewing interferes with eating, be sure to get proper dental care for your elderly parent. Even if she is in a nursing home or unable to get to the dentist, there are dentists available who do house calls and have mobile equipment. The nursing home should be able to assist you in arranging dental care for your elderly parent. To find dentists in the community who treat the elderly, you may be able to call your local dental society. Some elderly people unnecessarily live on pureed foods or foods that are easily chewed, merely because they do not have access to appropriate dental care. As caregivers, we must recognize the importance of the need for good dental care and help our elderly loved ones gain access to dental care on a regular basis.

Difficulty swallowing, which can result after a stroke, may rapidly lead to inadequate food intake. When food intake is insufficient due to the inability to swallow, the assistance of a physician, dietitian and/or speech therapist is essential. Swallowing evaluations and therapy to restore the swallowing mechanism may be necessary. If those interventions are not successful, the use of tube feeding may be suggested. Careful evaluation and consideration must be undertaken prior to the long term use of feeding tubes (as discussed in other chapters).

Difficulty digesting foods or stomach and abdominal discomfort may contribute to poor intake of food in your elderly parent. These problems should be evaluated by the physician and corrected, if possible, in order to maintain adequate nutrition. If your elderly parent has difficulty eating, ask why, and find out if upset stomach, heartburn, gas, or nausea interfere with eating patterns. Assist your parent in bringing these problems to her physician's attention.

Difficulty preparing meals may contribute to poor nutrition, especially if your elderly parent previously enjoyed cooking. Adapting the kitchen to her physical disabilities may aid in maintaining the ability to prepare meals, and it may actually enhance good eating habits. Adaptive can openers, bottle openers, cooking and eating utensils, bowls and other equipment are available through occupational therapists. If you believe that your elderly parent would benefit from maintaining the ability to cook, ask her physician to refer you to an occupational therapist who will come to the home and offer advice on preparing meals independently.

Perhaps the most important, yet least suspected, cause of altered appetite and nutrition is medications. As discussed in Chapter 6, the average elderly person may take anywhere from two to eight medications per day. Poor appetite, altered taste, stomach upset and imbalances of nutrients may be caused by certain medications, so every medication should be evaluated by the physician when poor appetite and nutrition are suspected. The benefits of continuing offending medications should be weighed against the negative effects on the nutritional status of your elderly loved one. For caregivers, being aware that medications may affect appetite and nutrition is important. You need not be an expert on medication side effects. You need only be aware that medications may affect appetite and nutritional status and to bring your awareness to the attention of your elderly parent's physician.

Vitamin deficiency may occur in your elderly parent, especially if adequate nutrition is not maintained or if certain disease states are present. Discuss vitamin supplementation with your elderly parent's physician, and ask for his suggestions. Supplementation of vitamins C, B and zinc may be necessary, especially if your elderly parent is recuperating from surgery or an illness. Vitamin D or calcium may be suggested by the physician for the treatment of osteoporosis. Be very careful not to supplement vitamins in your elderly parent without the advice of a physician, pharmacist and/or dietitian. Excessive doses of Vitamin D and other vitamins may actually have a harmful effect in an elderly person with altered physiology. In the elderly, more vitamins may not always mean better nutrition.

Nutritional supplements such as Ensure® are available in many flavors and often are good supplements to inadequate diets of the elderly. Ask your elderly parent's physician if a nutritional formula is necessary and which one he recommends. "Meals on Wheels" programs offer meals delivered to homebound elderly people and may be an option for your elderly parent. You can check with your local senior citizen center or Area Agency on Aging to see if "Meals on Wheels" programs are available in your elderly parent's service area. Senior nutrition sites may also offer hot meals to seniors in the community; often they are good for providing social interaction, as well as nutritious meals. Your local senior center or Area Agency on Aging may also provide locations and costs of such programs.

Proper nutrition throughout life is very important, and the caregiver who understands the nutritional needs and problems of the elderly will be better prepared to provide necessary assistance. If your elderly parent's physician is not aware of the nutritional needs of the elderly, don't give up. The average physician received little education in nutrition in medical school, and so his knowledge may be limited in that regard. Seek the assistance of a dietitian or a physician who specializes in nutrition and medicine. Most important, keep in mind that weight loss, poor appetite and decreased food intake may be an indication of a disease state in your elderly parent and should be thoroughly and promptly evaluated by a competent physician.

20

PREVENTION OF BEDSORES

PRESSURE SORES (DECUBITUS ULCERS)

A̲s DESCRIBED IN OTHER CHAPTERS of this book, prevention is a primary goal which the caregiver of an elderly parent should keep in mind. Prevention of bedsores is of utmost importance, yet most caregivers have little idea of how bedsores develop or of the significant impact they may have on the health and well-being of an elderly person.

The medical term for bedsore is decubitus, or pressure, ulcer. The term bedsore was probably originally used because of the association between the sores and their forming on people who are confined to a bed. The term bedsore is not entirely descriptive of the problem, because sores do not actually develop from being in bed. Bedsores develop from a combination of factors. Human tissue must have a constant supply of blood and nutrients; when pressure on tissue is unrelenting, this supply is interrupted and a pressure ulcer may form.

Have you ever slept in one position for too long and awakened to find that your skin was red in the area on which you slept? Most people have experienced this to some degree. After a few minutes, the redness goes away when you get up and move around. An elderly person who has impaired mobility and spends an excessive amount of time in one position may develop a pressure ulcer if not repositioned with assistance. Body tissue needs adequate blood supply to survive. Pressure upon body tissue over a period of time may cause blood flow to be interrupted and result in tissue death or development of bedsores. Development of bedsores depends upon the amount of pressure under which the tissue is placed, along with the amount of time the pressure is applied. It doesn't take much pressure or time for a frail, thin, elderly person to develop a bedsore. In fact, bedsores may develop within two hours of remaining in one position without being turned in bed or repositioned in a chair.

Certain parts of the body are more prone to developing pressure ulcers. These areas may include heels, coccyx (tail bone), sacrum, hips, shoulders, back, elbows or other places where bones may protrude. Bedsores are classified according to the severity of the damage done to tissue. There are four grades or stages of bedsores:

Stage One   surrounding tissue where pressure was applied becomes reddened;

Stage Two   the skin actually breaks open;

Stage Three the sore is deep enough to invade the underlying tissues;

Stage Four   the sore is so extensive that it extends deep into the muscle and possibly to the bone.

Once the bedsore has reached a stage three or four, it may take several months of uncomfortable, expensive treatment to heal. Some sores that reach these stages may never heal, especially if the elderly person is malnourished or suffering from cancer or other debilitating diseases.

Prevention of bedsores is of paramount importance, especially in the immobile, physically disabled elderly person for whom you may be providing care. It is much easier to prevent a bedsore than it is to heal it once it develops. Prevention includes a good understanding on the part of caregivers regarding what may lead to the development of bedsores.

Several factors, in addition to pressure, contribute to the cause of bedsores. Poor nutrition and chronic illness are two such factors. Many chronically ill elderly may not consume adequate calories, and malnutrition and depletion of protein stores may place them at a greater risk of developing bedsores. Elderly people who are incontinent of urine or feces may also be more prone to bedsore development because of the irritating effects that urine and feces may have on the skin. Elderly people with neurological deficits may not feel pain and discomfort as readily and may not be able to turn or reposition themselves in a bed or wheelchair. The combination of decreased sensation and immobility may lead to the development of bedsores. If you are caring for a frail, dependent, immobile, elderly loved one, just pulling her up in bed may contribute to bedsore development if not done properly. If a draw sheet or turn sheet is available, the sliding force or friction that contributes to skin breakdown may be avoided.

The treatment of bedsores is beyond the scope of this book.

Knowing how to treat them won't be necessary if you take preventive measures when caring for your elderly loved one. The following preventive steps may be helpful in preventing bedsores:

- Determine your loved one's ability to turn herself in bed or reposition herself in a chair. If she is unable to independently shift her weight or turn, assist her to do so at least every two hours.

- Avoid friction against the skin when pulling her up in a chair or bed. Be gentle. Avoid prolonged immobility.

- If skin is broken, consult a physician immediately and avoid further pressure on the area of broken skin.

- These preventive measures apply even if your loved one is in the hospital or nursing home. Don't rely on the nursing staff to turn or reposition your elderly, immobile loved one. Remind them, and be sure that it is being done.

Bedsores can develop quickly, especially in one who is acutely or chronically ill and in the hospital or nursing home. The use of physical restraints or other factors which restrict access to a bathroom (including the patient's physical limitations) may be common in these settings. If your loved one is not regularly turned and repositioned, bedsores can develop rapidly.

If your loved one is immobile due to paralysis or other musculo-skeletal problems, the use of protective and pressure reducing devices may be indicated. Sheepskin or foam heel protectors are available from the pharmacy or medical equipment supply and may reduce pressure on the heels. Special air or water mattresses, as well as gel and water filled wheelchair cushions, may also reduce pressure and help to prevent bedsores. If your loved one is immobile and you are caring for her in your home, be sure to get advice on bedsore prevention from her physician, nurse, social worker or physical therapist. If possible, try to assist your loved one, regularly, in walking or getting out of bed or the wheelchair. Prolonged sitting or lying in bed in one position creates a dangerous risk that should be avoided. Finally, be sure that adequate nutrition, hydration and medical care are provided to your loved one. There are very few areas in elder care where prevention is so important. Whether you are caring for an elderly parent at home or entrusting your parent's care to others, please ask for advice on the prevention of pressure ulcers, and make sure that this advice is followed.

21

UNDERSTANDING AND ADAPTING TO SENSORY LOSS

(CATARACT, GLAUCOMA, MACULAR DEGENERATION, DIABETIC RETINOPATHY)

 D ECLINES IN VISUAL AND HEARING ABILITIES are quite common in the elderly. Such declines may be associated with the normal aging process or may result from diseases that are common with advanced age. Caregivers who have an understanding of the sensory problems that accompany aging can be instrumental in aiding their elderly loved ones to improve and maintain quality of life. Knowledge of problems in vision and hearing will also be helpful in preventing premature disability, especially when it comes to prevention and treatment of diseases common to the aging eye.

Most of us take our eyesight and hearing for granted until difficulties develop. The loss of vision and hearing in an elderly person can be devastating, sometimes leading to increased dependence upon others for basic daily needs. Poor vision may prevent an elderly person from driving, preparing meals, reading, watching television, dressing, taking medications and even walking. Moreover, reduced vision may result in falls and motor vehicle accidents. That's why proper assessment and visual correction should be a high priority.

As one grows older the eye may undergo changes that affect vision. Many older people have difficulty with near vision that requires corrective lenses. Older people may also normally experience difficulties with light adaptation. More light may be required for good vision. Glare may become a problem, and it may take an elderly person longer to adjust when going out into bright sunlight or entering a dark room.

It is important that the caregiver assist in manipulating the home environment to compensate for the changes in vision that occur in an elderly loved one. Be sure that rooms in the home are adequately lit and that the lighting arrangement is without unnecessary glare. Night lights, hall lights, porch lights and lights in the bathroom may be left on for the safety of one who may arise at night to use the toilet. Glare can be avoided by not having shiny, highly polished floors in the house.

Remind your elderly loved one to not rush out from a dark to light area and to pause when coming in from bright sunlight. She should allow time for the pupil of the eye to adapt to the changes in light. Doing so may reduce the risk of falls and injury. Older people may also have difficulty distinguishing between colors. This can be particularly dangerous if medications are taken based upon their color. Greens and blues may be the most difficult for the aging eye to differentiate, so be sure that your elderly parent doesn't take her medications based upon color.

There are four common eye problems to which your aging parent or loved one may be susceptible. These are cataracts, glaucoma, macular degeneration, and diabetic retinopathy. Your knowledge of these eye problems will be instrumental in helping your elderly loved one receive proper medical attention. Regular eye examinations are very important for those in their later years. Ask your elderly loved one's family doctor for a referral to an ophthalmologist (eye doctor) at least every two years for a complete eye evaluation. If your loved one already has an eye disorder, more frequent visits to the ophthalmologist may be necessary.

Cataracts are commonly found in elderly people. A cataract is a clouding of the lens inside the eye, caused by changes in the proteins of the lens as one ages. Symptoms of cataracts may develop over months or even years. Symptoms of cataracts may include blurred or hazy vision, complaints of glare particularly at night, and difficulty with near or far vision. The treatment for cataracts is surgery, which usually involves the removal of the cataract and placement of a lens implant. Cataract surgery is not without risks or complications, but qualified surgeons may have very good success rates in restoring vision. Before agreeing to cataract surgery, one must take into account whether visual difficulties are interfering with activities of daily living. If cataracts are impairing your elderly parent's ability to function, cataract surgery may greatly improve quality of life.

Before choosing a cataract surgeon, check around to see if he is a board certified ophthalmologist with experience in cataract surgery. Ask your elderly parent's family doctor which ophthalmologist he would recommend, and check with your local medical society to see if the ophthalmologist is qualified. Cataract surgery is so commonplace these days that ophthalmologists can be aggressive in their marketing and advertising to seniors. Your job as a caregiver is to assist your elderly loved one in recognizing problems and gaining access to appropriate, necessary, qualified help.

While cataracts may develop over time and generally have recognizable symptoms and successful treatments, glaucoma can be a dangerous eye problem that often goes undetected and untreated until serious visual problems develop. Glaucoma is an eye disease that is the number one cause of blindness in this country. As one ages, the chances of getting glaucoma increase. Glaucoma is the result of abnormal pressure within the eye that causes damage to the optic nerve. In the initial stages of glaucoma, there may be no symptoms; this is why it is so important that you assist your elderly parent in obtaining routine eye examinations by an ophthalmologist. If your elderly parent complains of visual disturbances, do not simply assume that the complaints are a result of old age. Help your parent to see an eye doctor before the problem progresses and causes irreversible visual damage.

The two most common classifications of glaucoma of which caregivers should be aware are angle closure and open angle.

Angle closure glaucoma is less common, but if symptoms are recognized early it can be successfully treated. An attack of angle closure glaucoma can come on suddenly when the pressure in the eye rapidly increases. In an acute attack, your elderly loved one may suffer severe eye pain, nausea, vomiting, headache, and blurred vision. If you as a caregiver are not alert to the possiblity that these symptoms may stem from angle closure glaucoma, they may be mistaken for another illness unrelated to the eye. When such symptoms develop, it is a true medical emergency; if you do not get help from an ophthalmologist quickly, permanent blindness may develop. The treatment of acute angle closure glaucoma is surgery, along with medications to reduce the pressure within the eye.

Chronic open angle glaucoma is the typical type of glaucoma seen in the elderly and may be without symptoms until the later stages of the disease, when it causes a gradual loss of vision. Regular visits to the ophthalmologist are necessary to measure the pressure within the eye and to monitor treatment if glaucoma is present. The eye drops and medications used to treat glaucoma may have side effects, so they should be taken as directed. If your elderly parent needs such medications, be sure that she is able to take the eye drops properly. Sometimes difficulties in coordination, vision, and dexterity make self-administration of eye drops very difficult for an elderly person. If eye drops are prescribed, be sure that your elderly parent can self-administer them. If she can't, perhaps a neighbor, friend, or helper can be assigned the job. Discuss the treatment options with the ophthalmologist and be sure that your elderly loved one's general doctor is aware of the condition and in communication with the ophthalmologist. Also keep in mind that eye drops, even though they are instilled in the eye, can interact with medications taken by mouth. When you assist your elderly parent with visits to the doctor, be sure to take the eye drops, with her other medications, for him to review. Also, let your elderly parent's pharmacist know that eye drops are being used, so that he can check for drug interactions.

If your elderly loved one complains of problems with central vision, then macular degeneration may be suspected and an evaluation by an ophthalmologist is necessary. The macula is the central portion of the retina. In macular degeneration, peripheral vision may be spared, but difficulties in reading and watching television may occur. Even though treatment may be limited, close follow up by an ophthalmologist is essential.

Diabetic retinopathy (damage to the retina of the eye of diabetics) is a potential cause of blindness in people with diabetes. If your elderly parent suffers from diabetes, it is important that you assist her in maintaining control of blood sugar to prevent or delay the onset of diabetic retinopathy. As with other eye diseases, regular visits to the ophthalmologist are important. The caregiver whose elderly loved one is a diabetic should facilitate these visits and assist her in following the prescribed treatments.

In many cases, adjustment to reduced vision and the use of visual aides may be necessary for our elderly loved ones. Visual impairment is often associated with increased dependence upon caregivers. With your loved one, you should work through the significant emotional impact of her reduced vision. It is frightening to lose your vision at any age, and visual loss often leads to depression and isolation. If visual abilities cannot be restored, the caregiver should try to enhance remaining vision and adapt the elderly person's environment and activities to adjust to visual declines.

Safety of your visually impaired loved one is of utmost importance. Poor vision may lead to trips and falls, so be sure that the home is free of clutter, low lying tables, and other potential hazards. I suggest that you close your eyes and walk around your parent's home. In this way, you can discover what hazards exist, so that you can correct them. Often a visually impaired person has some degree of remaining vision. You may be able to enhance vision by adapting the environment and providing adaptive equipment.

Lighting is very important. If you increase the lighting in the home, vision may be enhanced. Halogen pole lamps that light up the whole room may be helpful. Providing extra light for specific tasks with a bright flashlight or desk light may also be helpful, but you should be sure that light is available throughout the room.

Along with increasing light in the environment, providing contrast between objects is important in enhancing vision. Providing contrast allows for the visually impaired person to recognize the difference between objects in the environment. For example, in reading, red letters on white paper may enhance vision, as opposed to blue letters on green paper or black letters on grey paper. These latter combinations provide less contrast and may make reading more difficult. A red toothbrush set on a white counter top may be easier to see than a white toothbrush on a white counter top, for an elderly person with visual impairment. A clear or white drinking cup placed on a white counter top may be more difficult to locate than a black or red cup on the same white counter. A cream or white light switch or plate mounted on a white wall may be more difficult to find than a red or black switch and wall plate on a white wall. If your elderly loved one is visually impaired, experiment with contrasts in the environment. Ask your elderly parent what contrasting materials she can see better, and adapt the environment based upon her abilities to see contrasts.

Along with lighting and contrasts, size of objects can influence vision. Often, the larger the object, the easier it is to identify. Of course, the size of an object is related to how close in space one is to the object. Objects on television may seem smaller, the farther away from the screen we go. A simple adjustment such as moving the television closer to your elderly loved one's favorite chair may enhance enjoyment of watching television, yet most of us wouldn't think of moving the television closer as a simple intervention. You can encourage your elderly loved one to move visual items closer and let her know that doing so is not a cause for embarrassment. Talking about feelings related to visual loss is important; try to encourage your elderly loved one to express herself. You should try to respond with empathy and encouragement.

In addition to bringing items in the environment closer to the eyes, another instrument for making them appear larger is magnification. I've seen magnification devices for low vision that range from a simple hand-held magnifier to an electronic reading machine utilizing closed circuit television technology. Anyone who is caring for a visually impaired person should seek the help of an optometrist or ophthalmologist specializing in low vision equipment. Have the specialist assist your elderly loved one in choosing magnifiers, and ask for assistance in learning their proper use. Also ask for referrals to local low vision support groups if they are available in your community. Get the number of the Braille Institute in your area and ask what type of assistance they offer. Often the Braille Institute or local libraries can assist you in finding books on tape or books with large print. Adaptive equipment such as phones with large numbers and "talking clocks" are also available and may help your loved one adapt to low vision. (See Resource Guide at the end of this book.)

Loss of hearing in the elderly can have a dramatic effect on social and daily activities. Many elderly people who have difficulty hearing may disengage and not participate in conversations, gatherings, watching television or recreational events. As a caregiver you should recognize hearing loss and work with your elderly loved one to optimize what hearing function is left. If your elderly loved one has difficulty hearing, check with her physician and get a referral to an audiologist (professional who specializes in hearing evaluation and prescription of assistive hearing devices). Be cautious of high pressure salespeople wanting to sell hearing aids to your elderly parent. Check with the doctor to see if something simple like impacted ear wax is causing difficulty in hearing.

Before investing in a hearing aid, be sure that your elderly parent really needs it and is capable of putting it on. I can't tell you how many elderly people with whom I work have hearing aids that just sit in the drawer or on the dresser because they are either embarrassed to wear them or can't insert them. A proper hearing evaluation, along with training in the use of a hearing aid, is essential. If your elderly loved one suffers from memory loss, be sure to check frequently to see where the hearing aid is. Often a memory impaired person will simply throw the hearing aid away or it will get lost in the bed linen. If possible, see if the hearing aid dispenser offers insurance for loss.

If hearing is impaired in your elderly loved one, please don't just attribute this loss to old age and not do anything to assist. Poor hearing is often associated with depression, and sometimes even paranoia, in the elderly. If your elderly loved one also suffers from low vision, the combination can really shut her off from the world. Check with the physician or audiologist about what organizations in your community offer assistance for the hearing impaired. These organizations may be able to help you locate assistive devices to enhance hearing for your elderly loved one. Most of these devices in some way amplify sound. The phone company or local Radio Shack may sell amplifiers that fit on the phone ear piece to enhance hearing. Phones, door bells, and smoke detectors with visual lights (which light up along with the sound) also may aid in daily functioning. Headphones that work with infrared or simple amplification may help in conversations and with watching television and listening to the radio. These devices are available in local electronic stores.

When you communicate with someone with a hearing impairment, it is not necessary to shout. Look directly at your elderly loved one and speak slowly, in a low tone, so that she can read your lips. If she cannot hear a word or phrase, choose a simpler, similar word or phrase until she understands you. If this doesn't work and if your elderly loved one can see well enough to read, write down what you are saying. Large rooms with poor acoustics and background noises from television or conversation makes communication with a hearing impaired person more difficult. Be sure that the room is quiet when you try to communicate. Try to be patient when communicating, no matter how frustrated you become. Our elderly loved ones with hearing impairments may be sensitive to our frustrations and cut off communication without letting their needs be known.

When I do training sessions with caregivers, I often do experiential role plays to let them know what it is like to live in an elderly person's body. This type of activity sensitizes caregivers and helps them to understand what their loved ones are going through. Try putting some cotton in your ears or wear some ear muffs for an hour or so. While doing this, take some Vaseline and smear it on your favorite pair of glasses and wear them for an hour. See what you bump into, and feel what it's like to not hear. See how your family reacts when you put the television on too loud or when you ignore them when they are talking to you. Living in a world of silence and darkness can be scary. Remember to touch when you communicate with one who has sensory impairments. Even if you are not seen or heard, the touch of your hand—and heart—may be comforting.

22

COPING WITH PARKINSON'S DISEASE

ONE OF THE MOST COMMON neurological diseases affecting the elderly is Parkinson's disease. Because of the progressive dependence and disability associated with Parkinson's, the caregiver may experience a substantial burden of care.

A cause for Parkinson's disease has not yet been established, but there is a fair understanding of the chemical changes in the brain of a victim that lead to the disabling symptoms. Two chemicals in the brain seem to be out of balance in the Parkinson's patient. These two chemicals are acetylcholine and dopamine. While there is not a cure for Parkinson's disease, treatment is generally geared toward maintaining normal concentrations of these two chemicals in the brain.

The severity and course of Parkinson's disease can vary from one individual to another. The initial symptom a caregiver may notice is a tremor or shaking in one or both of an elderly loved one's hands or arms. The shaking generally occurs when the arm or hand is at rest. Other symptoms may include muscle stiffness and rigidity, slowed movement, stooping or hunched posture, difficulty initiating walking, trouble with balance, a shuffling type of walk, expressionless facial features, and changes in speech quality. As symptoms worsen, difficulties in swallowing, eating, and managing basic activities of daily living may develop. A number of Parkinson's patients may develop changes in memory or personality as the disease progresses; these changes may lead to difficulties for the patient, family and caregiver.

If you notice any of the above symptoms developing in your elderly loved one, seek the advice of a physician. If necessary, a referral to a neurologist (specialist in diseases of the nervous system) may be necessary. Developing a good relationship with the physician is paramount for the caregiver and patient faced with Parkinson's disease. Close and frequent communication may be necessary with the physician in order to adjust doses of medication and prevent side effects. Choose a physician who is accessible and willing to take the time to help you understand this disease. Follow the physician's instructions very carefully when administering medications. Don't change doses or administration times, and don't start and stop medications for Parkinson's without the advice of the physician. Doing so may worsen symptoms and cause unnecessary disability for your loved one.

Several medications are used to treat the symptoms of Parkinson's disease. Depending on the severity of symptoms, course of illness, and side effects experienced, the drugs may be used alone or in combination. Anticholinergic drugs may be used early in the disease to regulate the balance of the brain chemical acetylcholine. Many of these drugs are similar in make-up to antihistamines and may have side effects, particularly in the elderly. Dry mouth, nervousness, dizziness, difficulty with urination, changes in mood, and visual disturbances are just a few of the side effects your loved one may experience while taking anticholinergic medications. Be sure that you alert the physician to any side effects. Let him know if your loved one takes any other medications, including over-the-counter medications, so that he can see if there are any potential drug to drug interactions.

The primary treatment of Parkinson's disease is geared toward increasing the brain's usable supply of dopamine, the chemical that is insufficient in the brains of Parkinson's patients. Dopamine levels of the brain are manipulated by taking the drug levodopa or a combination of carbidopa and levodopa, called Sinemet®. By combining carbidopa and levodopa, the dosage of levodopa can be reduced, thus relieving some uncomfortable side effects. There is some evidence that levodopa loses its effectiveness after prolonged use, so some neurologists may wait until the Parkinson's symptoms are serious enough before starting treatment. As with all drugs used to treat Parkinson's, side effects can become a problem. Side effects of levodopa therapy may include hallucinations, confusion, changes in mood, poor appetite, changes in vision, and other side effects associated with the kidneys, stomach, intestines and heart. Because of the potential side effects of drugs used to treat Parkinson's, as mentioned earlier, it is essential that the physician be consulted before changing the medication regimen.

Other drugs used to treat Parkinson's may include amantadine (Symmetrel®) and bromocriptine (Parlodel®). These medications also have side effects and should be taken with great care. I recommend that all caregivers of Parkinson's patients take time to research and understand the action and side effects of Parkinson's medications. Your doctor and pharmacist can be instrumental in your education. You may also go to the local book store or library to find several books on Parkinson's disease that outline in more detail the medications discussed above.

Proper use of medications is important in the treatment of Parkinson's disease, but the caregiver should not forget the basics of good care of an elderly loved one. Safety and efforts to prevent falls and hazards in the home are essential. A home safety visit by a physical therapist and education on proper exercises to maintain mobility, flexibility and balance may assist in the patient's well-being. Proper nutrition and adequate fluids are important for the Parkinson's patient; recognizing early signs of acute illness, as outlined in other chapters, can be life saving.

Because of the progressive, often protracted nature of this affliction, caregivers would be wise to seek help from support groups and any other available means of assistance. Other chapters describe the nature of the caregiving relationship, as well as the types of support services and living arrangements available for the elderly in need of help. For information about Parkinson's disease and available help, you should contact the Parkinson's support organizations listed in the Resource Guide at the end of this book.

23

CANCER IN THE ELDERLY

T HE ELDERLY AS A WHOLE may be at greater risk of developing cancer than the general population. Moreover, the chances of successful treatment and cure for an elderly cancer patient may be reduced. A comprehensive description of the treatment for cancer in the elderly is beyond the scope of this book. The goal of this chapter is to inform the caregiver about the importance of early detection of cancer in elderly parents and loved ones. Often, early detection of cancer increases the likelihood of cure and reduces the burden of illness. I have worked with many elderly patients suffering with various forms of cancer. Cancer can be devastating to the patient and family, and while there may not always be cures, the importance of early detection cannot be stressed too much as an important responsibility of the caregiver. Common sites for cancer in the elderly include the colon, lung, breast, prostate, bladder, and cervix. Cancer in the elderly may be diagnosed at later stages than cancer in the young, because symptoms may be falsely associated with normal declines of aging. In addition, health care professionals may not be as vigilant in preventive cancer screening in the elderly.

Discuss with your elderly loved one's physician what early cancer detection screens he believes to be necessary, at least on an annual basis. At a minimum, suggest that there be an annual breast examination and a breast mammography as necessary. You may even want to encourage your elderly mother to perform regular self-breast examinations. Early detection of breast cancer increases the likelihood of survival, even in an elderly woman, yet elderly women and physicians caring for them may not recognize the importance. In addition to breast examinations, pap smears to detect cervical cancer in an early stage should be performed regularly. If you ask your elderly mother when she last had a pap smear and pelvic examination, you may be surprised to find out that the answer is, "Never," or, "A very long time ago." Ask the doctor how often he recommends a pelvic exam and pap smear for patients over sixty-five years of age, and encourage your elderly mother to follow the doctor's recommendations. If her personal physician recommends little or no cancer screening, you may seek a second or third opinion from a gynecologist or oncologist. The National Cancer Institute Cancer Information Service may also offer recommendations and can be reached at 1-800-4-CANCER.

Cancer of the colon may be detected early by encouraging your elderly parent to have stool tests for occult blood at least annually. Occult blood is blood that is passed through the intestine that cannot be seen with the naked eye. Intestinal bleeding, either occult or visible, may be a sign of colon cancer. The test for occult blood can be done with a very simple home test provided by the physician. Early detection of colon cancer, even in the elderly, can save lives.

Cancer of the prostate in men is common, so encourage your elderly father to have annual rectal examinations so that prostate cancer might be detected early. Your job as a caregiver will be much easier if you are an advocate for your elderly parent with health care providers. It is much easier to discuss these issues and encourage prevention than it is to care for an elderly parent with terminal cancer—cancer that might have been recognized and treated effectively, if it had been detected at an early stage.

Whether cancer of the lung is detected early depends on the type of screening and early detection method, especially if your elderly parent is or was a smoker. An abnormal cough with unusual mucous production should be brought to the attention of the physician. Unexplained weight loss, poor appetite and generalized weakness should also be brought to the attention of the physician.

Cancer of the skin is also common in the elderly, especially those who have had prolonged sun exposure during their lives. Regular body examinations should be performed by a general physician or dermatologist in order to detect skin cancer at an early stage. Skin growths with irregular borders, varying colors and changes in size may be suspicious and should be evaluated. Often, skin cancer may not be detected at an early stage because an elderly person may not be able to see well or may not have the flexibility to visually check hard-to-reach body parts. It is imperative, therefore, to assist your elderly loved one in having regular skin check-ups.

If cancer is diagnosed in your elderly loved one, you will need to provide emotional support and, possibly, physical support and assistance. Old age alone is not a reason to withhold treatment. Cancer treatment in the elderly should be discussed and planned on an individual basis; the patient and the family should be included in discussions of treatment options. Quality of life issues, as well as benefits versus side effects of treatments, should be discussed. Care to relieve pain and discomfort is essential, even if everyone agrees not to treat the cancer. For more information on cancer treatments and options, you can contact the National Cancer Institute, 9000 Rockville Pike, Bethesda, MD 20892, or call the Cancer Information Service at 1-800-4-CANCER.

24

COPING WITH
ARTHRITIS AND PAIN

ARTHRITIS MAY BE COMMON to the elderly; painful, stiff joints may lead to immobility and reduced independence.

Two common forms of arthritis are osteoarthritis and rheumatoid arthritis. Osteoarthritis may be less disabling than rheumatoid arthritis; the typical symptoms are painful joints. Rheumatoid arthritis may cause severe joint deformities and inflammation of joints to the point that performing basic activities is limited.

If your elderly loved one experiences pain due to arthritis, you may need not only to assist in obtaining an appropriate evaluation, but also to monitor treatment. A rheumatologist is a medical doctor specializing in the treatment of arthritis. If you wish to assist your elderly loved one to see a rheumatologist, be sure that her family doctor is aware of this and stays involved. As mentioned in other chapters, when treating the elderly it is particularly important to keep the whole person and picture in mind; the family doctor should act as the facilitator.

Pain relief, appropriate exercise, good nutrition, proper sleep, physical therapy and emotional support are all valuable modalities in treating the elderly person with arthritis. The goal may be to reduce pain and disability while allowing the elderly arthritic to maintain as much functional independence as possible.

Pain relief is best accomplished when medications are taken properly. Discuss in detail with your elderly loved one's physician the proper use of pain- and inflammation-reducing medications. Pain medication should be taken as directed, and it may be less effective if it is taken after the pain is present. Pain causes anxiety, and anxiety further aggravates pain. Therefore it may be more beneficial to take pain medicine on a regular basis to avoid periods of pain. Caution in taking pain medication is essential, because of potential side effects. Serious side effects such as bleeding ulcers may develop when taking certain pain medications. Discuss this potential side effect with the physician, so that this problem can be avoided.

One of the problems that arthritis may cause in the elderly is reduced mobility. If pain is present and the pain is relieved by rest, an elderly arthritic may limit activity. One must be cautious not to limit activity to the point that severe deconditioning results. For this reason, I recommend that a physical therapist be involved in instructing elderly arthritis patients about coping with arthritis, so that they can remain as active and independent as possible. An occupational therapist may also be of assistance if your elderly loved one requires adaptive equipment to perform basic daily activities. You should seek such referrals from the family physician and/or rheumatologist. Other information about arthritis may be obtained by contacting the local arthritis foundation listed in your area phone directory.

25

OSTEOPOROSIS

(BONE LOSS)

OSTEOPOROSIS IN THE ELDERLY is a disorder characterized by loss of bone mass and strength. The result of osteoporosis in the elderly may be bone fractures and disability. Osteoporosis is more common in white, elderly women with thin body frames and is a serious concern for the elderly and their caregivers.

Vitamins and hormones to treat osteoporosis may be less beneficial in the elderly. Ideally, preventive treatment with estrogen replacement should be started within a few years after menopause. Vitamin D and calcium supplementation may also be prescribed for post-menopausal women who are at risk of developing osteoporosis.

Care should be taken to prevent heavy lifting, falls, and other risks of fracturing bone. In some elderly people with osteoporosis, I have seen fractures occur merely because of their sitting down too abruptly or turning in bed. If your elderly loved one experiences the sudden onset of pain in a joint or bone, seek medical advice to evaluate a fracture predisposed by osteoporosis, even if a fall or accident did not precipitate the pain.

Treatment of osteoporosis should be individualized to the elderly person, and I suggest that you seek the advice of your elderly loved one's physician to discuss whether osteoporosis is present and how and if he wishes to treat it.

26

PROBLEMS WITH THE HEART AND BLOOD PRESSURE

As WE AGE, OUR HEARTS AND BLOOD VESSELS undergo changes related to aging and disease. An elderly person may experience chest pain (angina), irregularities of heart rhythm, congestive heart failure, high blood pressure, and many other difficulties of the heart and circulatory system.

Regular check-ups by a physician to control and monitor heart disorders, as well as high blood pressure, are essential in the elderly patient.

Blood pressure can be defined as the pressure which blood pumped by the heart places upon the arteries. When the heart contracts (systole), the first or top blood pressure reading is taken (systolic pressure). In the resting phase of the heart beat (diastole), the diastolic pressure is measured. Normal blood pressure is difficult to define in the elderly, and the typical "normal blood pressure" of 120/80 may not apply to older adults. As one ages, the arteries may lose elasticity and the result may be high blood pressure. High blood pressure may be caused by a number of factors, alone or in combination. Blood pressures in the elderly may be considered abnormal if the systolic (top number) is above 160 and the diastolic (bottom number) is above 90. Blood pressure can vary with different readings and under different conditions. Often, just a visit to the doctor's office can raise blood pressure, due to the anxiety present during the visit. This phenomenon is termed white coat hypertension. If your elderly loved one has high blood pressure, medications may be prescribed by the physician. Purchasing a home blood pressure device (sphygmomanometer) may assist you in helping your elderly loved one monitor blood pressure; sharing this information with the physician may help with the treatment of your loved one. Medications to treat blood pressure may have side effects, so discuss the risks, benefits and potential side effects with the physician and follow his directions closely. (See Chapter 6.)

If your elderly parent suffers from congestive heart failure, you should be vigilant in monitoring treatment and recognizing early signs of distress. Acute congestive heart failure can be treated with success, especially if treatment is initiated promptly. Chronic heart failure can also be treated with proper use of medications. Signs to watch for and immediately report to the physician include: difficulty breathing, sudden increase in pulse rate, difficulty lying flat in bed (often an elderly person will prop herself up with pillows at night because of difficulty breathing when lying flat), coughing with or without bringing up blood, blue lips or nail beds, shortness of breath with or without exertion, retaining of fluid with weight gain, swollen legs, and the sudden onset of unexplained confusion. Any of these signs, whether they develop quickly or progress slowly, should be reported to the physician immediately. Again I must emphasize that early detection and proper management of illness in the elderly is of great importance, even if a cure is not possible.

Heart attacks (myocardial infarction) may result when oxygen rich blood is prevented from reaching the heart muscle, usually due to occluded coronary arteries. Angina or transient chest pain which lasts a short period of time may be a symptom of heart disease and may occur more frequently upon exertion in stressful situations, after heavy meals, or in cold weather. If your elderly loved one complains of chest pain, a thorough evaluation should be done by a physician. Often a nitroglycerin pill under the tongue or a nitroglycerin patch applied to the skin is used to dilate blood vessels and alleviate chest pain. Be sure to assist your elderly loved one in taking angina and heart medications properly, and if chest pain persists, seek prompt emergency medical attention. Remember that an elderly person may or may not show the classic signs of a heart attack (such as chest pain and tightness, nausea, sweating, and pain down the left arm).

The chances are pretty good that if you are caring for an elderly parent or loved one, he or she may at some point develop a heart problem. This book is not intended to give detailed descriptions of heart ailments in the elderly. As with other areas in elder care, the caregiver should assist elderly loved ones in accessing good medical care and in safely following the instructions of the physician.

27

DIABETES

THE CHANCES OF DEVELOPING DIABETES or glucose intolerance may be increased in the elderly. In diabetes there may be a reduction in the amount of insulin produced in the pancreas, or the insulin produced may have less effect in facilitating the transfer of glucose in the blood to cells and tissues of the body. Diabetes can be classified as insulin dependent (injectable insulin required for treatment) or non-insulin dependent (injectable insulin not required). Symptoms of diabetes in the elderly may include:

- increased urination or thirst,
- weight loss with or without increased appetite,
- slow healing of wounds and
- increased susceptibility to infections.

The doctor may order blood and urine tests to verify high blood sugar and diabetes. If the diagnosis is established, you may need to assist your loved one in carrying out the treatment plan, including medications, dietary interventions and regular check-ups. Because of problems associated with diabetes related to the blood vessels, good preventive care is necessary. Regular foot check-ups to prevent wound infections are essential, because often, feeling in the foot is lost with diabetes. If a wound becomes infected, amputation of a toe or foot may become necessary. Regular eye check-ups are also necessary, so that the doctor can look for damage to the retina, which can be caused by diabetes.

If your loved one develops diabetes, you may be instrumental in monitoring care. Discuss with the doctor various treatments, as well as how to recognize diabetic emergencies. Home monitoring of blood sugar may be suggested; this can be done with a glucose monitoring machine, bought at the drug store. In treating diabetes, patient education and careful following of medical instructions are very important. If your loved one has diabetes, keep a close eye on the condition and learn about appropriate care.

28

HYPOTHERMIA

Whole HYPOTHERMIA MAY BE INFREQUENT in the elderly, I think it is worth brief mention because of the potential danger and the ease of prevention. Elderly people may be at an increased risk of developing hypothermia (body temperature below 95°F) for a variety of reasons. Difficulty in self-regulation of body temperature may occur because of:

- various medications,
- inability to regulate a thermostat,
- inability to recognize cold,
- the home's being poorly insulated or heated,
- confusion,
- certain disease states.

Whatever the possible cause, adult children of aging parents should be alert to the possibility of hypothermia, particularly if an elderly parent lives in a colder climate.

Temperatures of 60°F or below can cause hypothermia; the results can be deadly. Be sure the heat in your parent's house is working and that your parent is able to see and operate the thermostat controls. Often, elderly people may not turn on the heat because they want to save on heating bills. Perhaps this is a result of their growing up in the depression. Whatever the reason, be sure to encourage your parents to keep the thermostat at least at 70°F and dress warmly in colder months, both inside and outside the house. Signs of hypothermia may include confusion, sleepiness, cool skin and body temperature measured at below 95°F.

This is a medical emergency. Rewarming should be done under close supervision at a hospital. Rapid rewarming may cause severe medical complications. If you suspect hypothermia, wrap your elderly loved one in a blanket and warm coat and take her to the closest emergency room. Prevention is much more successful than treatment, so keep the possibility of accidental cold exposure in your mind, especially during the winter months.

29

CARE NEAR THE END OF LIFE

ETHICAL AND SURROGATE DECISION MAKING

T HE RIGHT TO DIE! Years ago, death and dying had very little to do with rights. Grandmother became ill and the doctor was summoned to the bedside at home to comfort the patient and family. Nature had its way. The family grieved and life went on. In today's sophisticated, medically technical and legal environment, nature is challenged every day. The human body can be kept alive at all costs, despite the absence of a functioning mind and spirit. We can keep people "alive" with ventilators and tube feedings for several years, with absolutely no hope for a meaningful recovery or quality of life.

The decisions to withhold or withdraw life sustaining therapy are ethically complicated and highly emotional. In the past, many of these decisions were either not necessary, due to lack of invasive treatment procedures, or not discussed with us as patients. In medicine of old, the physician was the ultimate, angelic decision maker whose opinion was never questioned. The patient simply did what the doctor ordered. In many instances a patient with terminal cancer was not even told of the diagnosis, because the physician thought this knowledge would interfere with treatment outcomes.

The evolving trend in today's medical world is to involve the patient in decisions affecting care and quality of life. The right to self-determination is the key ingredient in any ethical life and death situation that may arise. The choice of whether to extend life, or in many cases prolong death, should be left up to the patient, family or concerned surrogate decision makers. The physician and medical staff's role is to educate, counsel and guide patients and families through this difficult time. The physician should explain fully the proportionate risks and benefits of life sustaining and life prolonging therapy, so that the patient and family can make an informed decision.

Often we as caregivers become surrogate decision makers for our loved ones, because they are unable to make informed decisions, due to severe illness or cognitive impairments. As stressed in other chapters, planning ahead is the number one rule in the mission of a caregiver.

Before a life and death decision has to be made, it is imperative that you discuss advance wishes and directives with your elderly parent and her physician. Not doing this can be very costly and devastating to an elderly person and family, as illustrated in the following scenario. This scene is played out daily in hospitals and nursing homes throughout this country.

Her name was Sara. At 90 her eyes still had a blue sparkle. Her silver hair reflected beams of the morning sun, as it shone through the window by her bed. During my daily rounds in the nursing home, when I entered her room I would look at the pictures on Sara's walls; they told her life story. A life of dedication to her family was evident by a portrait of Sara and her seven children, brought to this country to escape persecution in Russia. This old, tattered, family portrait had survived along with Sara, throughout the years. Although Sara had lost so much of her physical health and being throughout the years, the sparkle in her eyes, shown so clearly in the portrait, could still be seen.

As I would look around the room, the pictures—when examined in chronological order—slowly blossomed from black and white into color. It was a pictorial history of a family of seven children, twelve grandchildren, and five great grandchildren.

I remember the day Sara was admitted. Coming to a nursing home had been a difficult decision for Sara and her family to make. Sara, proud and stoic, did not want her children burdened with her care.

Sara adjusted well, and her life revolved around visits from the family. The nursing home staff, aware of the JOY Sara's family brought, reminded her of family visits when she was down and depressed. Sara was paralyzed on one side and could no longer walk, but she was a delight to see with her great grandchildren. They melted in her arms and were so proud to share with Sara their school projects, art work and awards. To them, Sara—or "Bubby" as they called her—meant unconditional love and approval. Even in Sara's poor health, her children and grandchildren saw her as a source of strength and love in times of trouble. Sara was immortal in the eyes of her family, and matters of life and death were never discussed. Nobody knew what Sara's wishes on life and death treatment were, and everyone just assumed that everything would work itself out should a crisis arise.

Unfortunately, early one Sunday morning, Sara's condition dramatically changed. She appeared to have had another stroke, and she was transferred to the acute hospital for further evaluation and treatment. While in the emergency room, Sara's heart stopped, and she was vigorously resuscitated and put on a ventilator to assist her respiration. Because Sara could no longer swallow or eat, a feeding tube was placed down her nose to provide fluids and nutrition. When Sara's family visited, she was unaware of their presence. They sat at her bed and wept, while taking turns holding her hand.

After six days of this pain and suffering, the doctor asked Sara's family what Sara's treatment wishes would have been, had she been still able to make an informed decision. Nobody in the family knew, because it hadn't been discussed with Sara. It was left for the family to decide whether the treatment, with ventilation and tube feedings, should be continued.

Sara's family was shocked, stunned and, more disturbingly, ill prepared to make such a tremendous decision. They knew in their hearts that Sara would not have wanted to live in such a vegetative state, but nobody knew what to do, and nobody wanted the responsibility of making the decision. The family struggled for three days, as Sara's condition declined. On the ninth day after Sara's stroke, it was decided by the majority of the family to withdraw the assisted ventilation but to continue the tube feedings. Three children did not agree with the decision to remove the ventilator, and one child thought all life support should be discontinued. These differences in opinion brought even more stress to a family already in crisis.

With the family at Sara's bedside, the ventilator was disconnected. Much to everyone's surprise, Sara spontaneously began to breath again. The family seemed both relieved and grief-stricken with every breath that Sara took. While in the hospital, Sara developed pneumonia and several other complications that required painful, costly invasive interventions. After a twenty-eight day hospitalization, Sara was discharged back to the nursing home. When Sara arrived, the nursing home staff were saddened by what they saw. Sara looked like a totally different person. Her face was drawn, and she had lost a tremendous amount of weight. The only recognizable sign of life left in Sara was the sparkle in her eye, which remained with her throughout her life. Sara required constant, round the clock attention from the nursing home staff. She had a tube in her bladder to collect urine, a tube in her nose to feed her, and a diaper on for when she would move her bowels. While in the hospital, Sara had developed a bedsore, due to lack of movement; it required daily treatment. Sara was dependent upon the nursing staff for every daily need. They turned her, cleaned her, bathed her, moved her limbs for her, and gave her medications for pain and discomfort.

Somehow Sara kept pulling out the nourishment tube from her nose. She could not swallow, and attempts to feed her were fruitless. With the little strength Sara had, she would pull on her tube, trying to remove the only source of nourishment that maintained her life. Because the tube was constantly being displaced, it was decided that Sara's only functional limb would be restrained with a mitten and soft tie, which would be removed every two hours for comfort and circulation. Visits from Sara's family began to drop off after several weeks, since it was very difficult for them to see her in this condition and she had no idea who was in the room with her, anyhow. The adults in the family wanted the great grandchildren to have only fond memories of Sara, so they never brought them in to visit anymore. It seemed as though Sara and her family were suffering a living death. Sara was uncomfortable and had no quality left to her life. Each time her feeding tube was displaced, it was replaced with yet another. After three months of this suffering, it was discussed and decided by the family that the feeding tube was not in Sara's best interest. Sara had no hope for recovery and would not have wanted to live in such a state. The next time Sara pulled her feeding tube out, it would not be replaced. Sara would be kept comfortable and be allowed to die with dignity.

The day before she died, I knew that my visit would probably be the last that I would make while Sara was with us on this earth. During the three years that she had been my patient, I had known her in times of happiness and sorrow. I also knew in my heart, as did Sara's family, that it was her time to depart this world and for her beautiful spirit to be committed to the hands of God.

Comfortable, and surrounded by her family, Sara died the next morning. I attended Sara's memorial service, where the glory of her life was shared with all those present. Indeed, Sara was a great woman, with a great family. It was a true gift to be part of her caregiving, as a professional. Sara's family, through their struggle, learned a valuable lesson about life and death and decisions surrounding these issues. As a whole, they believe that they had made the correct choices for Sara. Had they been prepared in advance, Sara and her family might not have had to endure the hardships they did for nearly four months.

When we are young and strong, many of us feel immortal. Even all the death and violence we see on television and in the movies probably doesn't make us ponder our mortality. When we are young and have much to live for, the thought of death may be frightening and bring sadness. I have found in working with older people, that most of the time a very old person doesn't view death the way a younger person does. To an older person, death is a natural process that is expected and, often, welcomed. Many elderly people whom I counsel tell me that they want to die. They feel that they have outlived friends and spouses, and they are lonely. They feel that they have outlived the usefulness of their body. Often chronic pain, multiple hospitalizations, and the inability to take care of oneself may precipitate the wish to die. Many elderly people just have a natural peace about them when it comes to death. Some look forward to being with God in Heaven and enjoying a reunion with loved ones they have lost.

The death of a child is tragic. No matter how hard we try, it is difficult to find reason for any child's being stricken with a deadly disease or killed in an accident. The death of an adult is difficult because emotionally and financially dependent people may be left behind. No matter what the age of a person, at death someone will feel the loss of love and companionship. With the very old, it may be our responsibility as caregivers to help them through the process of dying, just as we help a child adjust to the process of living.

How do we as caregivers help prepare our loved ones for death? Fortunately, many elderly people are more comfortable with the subject than their adult children are. I often witness the elderly parent consoling the adult child when it comes to discussing the death of the elderly person. However, we do need to offer counsel and support to our elderly loved ones and patients who are dying. If I had a seedling for every elderly person with whom I have worked who has told me that she or he wants to die, I could plant a whole forest. Communication is of the utmost importance, so that everyone in the family can gain closure on life and death issues.

Many times I have witnessed incidents in which one of my patients in the nursing home would be near death and we would notify the adult children. The children would come at the last minute to say goodbye, and many times they would be too late. The elderly parent, before death, would have shared with the staff the things that she wished she could have disclosed or said to her children. The adult children would not have gotten the chance to hear from her or to say what they wanted to tell their elderly parent before death. Often in such cases, the children are left with anger and guilt.

When your parents are elderly, you never know which goodbye will be the last. Don't wait until it's too late to share your feelings and to get closure on the life you have shared so long with your elderly parent.

Death is a unique experience for every human being. Like birth, however, death is a process that all life commonly shares. What causes death? Well, some people die of cancer. Some people die of heart and lung disease. Some people die of infections. Some people die from accidents. Some take their own lives. Some people have their lives taken by others. No matter what the doctor writes on the death certificate as the cause of death, the real cause of death in all cases is BIRTH. Whoever is born shall die. I haven't met anyone yet who can dispute this fact. Once we understand and accept the fact that death is a natural part of life, we can assist ourselves and our elderly loved ones in dealing with mortality.

Many people have described the emotional feelings associated with death and dying. Professionals discuss death as a process with many stages, including denial, anger, bargaining, grief and acceptance. These stages may be delineated in a younger person who is diagnosed with a fatal illness. You may not see such stages in your ninety-year-old parent who is facing death; perhaps these stages were spread out over such a long period of time that they are not readily apparent. What do you say to your ninety-year-old parent when you visit and she says, "I want to die"? Many caregivers argue with the elderly person and say something like, "Come on, you don't want to die! Look at all the grandchildren and family you have to live for. We love you and want you with us."

In a sense, these types of responses are meant to comfort your elderly parent; however, in reality, you may be invalidating a legitimate feeling your parent has. Maybe the elderly person doesn't feel that life is worth living. It is my experience that no matter how hard you try to convince an elderly person of how much there is left to live for, it doesn't do much good. Instead of arguing about the value of life left, try to deal with the feeling of wanting to die. Respond by saying something like, "I understand that you want to die. How do you feel about death? Is it scary? Is there anything left in life you want to do before death? What do you think happens after you die? How can we help you prepare for death?"

Questions similar to these help the elderly person to express true feelings and may aid the family in dealing with issues prior to death. It is O.K. to talk about death. Talking about it won't hurt your elderly parent. As a matter of fact, you may even wish to bring the subject up if you feel your elderly parent is uncomfortable doing so. During these discussions, be sure to cover your parent's belief systems regarding life sustaining therapy. With today's medical technology, death can become an ethical issue for many elderly people. We have the technology today to keep people "alive," regardless of the quality of life. In many cases it is, indeed, a question of quantity versus quality of life.

Life and death are very personal issues, so it is difficult to direct care based on individual preferences and belief systems of medical professionals. The wishes of your elderly parent, who is the patient, should weigh utmost in everyone's mind when life and death decisions are to be made. The problem is that often the wishes of the elderly person were never discussed in advance. When death is imminent, the patient may not be competent to make her own decisions; they are made for her by family or health professionals. We hope and pray that the decisions that are made on behalf of our elderly parents reflect what they truly want. To be sure that we know what an elderly parent's wishes are regarding life sustaining therapy, we should have discussions far before the issue comes up. To be sure that your elderly parent's feelings are known, assist her in filling out advanced directives that outline what she wants done in a life and death situation.

There are written instruments available that outline, specifically, what we want done in the event of an incurable illness or if death is imminent. Most of these documents can be completed at no cost and with little professional assistance. These advanced directives include the durable power of attorney for health care, the advanced directive to physicians, and living wills. Different states may have varying regulations governing such documents, so it would be wise to check with your physician or local medical association for more information and for availability of these documents.

The Durable Power of Attorney for Health Care is a document that gives written permission for a particular person to make health care decisions for a patient, in the event that the patient is not competent to do so. It is important to note that the elderly person must be competent when she executes a durable power of attorney for health care. The document becomes effective upon incapacitation, at which time the appointed decision maker or "agent" can express the wishes of the loved one. You can usually obtain a durable power of attorney document at no cost from a physician, hospital, social work agency, library, stationary store or local medical society. There is no need for a lawyer to complete the document with you, despite the impression given by the word attorney in the durable power of attorney. You should, however, sit down with your elderly parent and her doctor to specifically discuss the benefits and drawbacks of life sustaining therapy. For you and your parent to make informed decisions, it is important to have some understanding about what life sustaining therapy actually entails.

Life sustaining therapy can mean any number of things to different lay people and medical professionals. Intravenous antibiotics to fight an infection in a ninety-year-old, terminally ill patient, may be considered life sustaining and extraordinary to some people, yet necessary and expected therapy to others. What is life sustaining depends upon the value systems of the person being treated and the people doing the treatments. What is difficult with advanced discussions of these matters is that one cannot always anticipate what future circumstances may develop with advanced age and terminal illness. Medicine is not an exact science, so making predictions about recovery and results of procedures is not always one hundred percent accurate.

When completing a durable power of attorney for health care, you should explicitly understand and discuss certain conditions and write what your wishes are in the blank spaces. Ask your doctor to outline several scenarios based upon his experience of working with elderly people. At a minimum, discuss the following:

- receiving cardiopulmonary resuscitation (CPR)
- being hospitalized
- undergoing surgery
- being placed on a ventilator
- being fed through a tube
- receiving intravenous antibiotics or fluids if death is imminent

Cardiopulmonary resuscitation (CPR) is a procedure used when a person's heart and breathing ceases. It can be very successful in bringing back life to younger people and to older people who are healthy and strong. If done properly, with the proper equipment at hand, CPR saves lives. In a very old person with multiple medical problems, CPR is not very often successful. When CPR is successful in these cases, the person is often left with a very poor quality of life and may even remain in a coma or chronic vegetative state. You need to ask yourself and your elderly parents if they want to take a chance by allowing CPR—the chance of whether they will be brought back to *just life* or quality life. Most people with whom I work don't want to be resuscitated if their hearts stop, and we respect their wishes. Very few want everything possible done, but for those who do, we abide by their advance directives also.

The question you need to ask yourself in deciding about life sustaining therapy is this: do the treatments outweigh the possible benefits of the therapy? What results will the treatment bring in terms of cure or quality of life? If, for example, your elderly parent has terminal illness but is not near death, a procedure that will relieve pain may be beneficial. If her heart stops, CPR may not be beneficial. The other question that is often raised is: What is the definition of quality of life? I've had patients who can't walk or feed themselves as a result of a stroke, who still want to live, feeling that there is quality to their lives. I have had other patients who can take care of themselves, but due to loneliness or depression, feel that there is no life quality and would not want resuscitation in the event of a cardiac arrest. These situations are all very personal and subjective, and they require significant discussions prior to a problem's arising.

Many times in these discussions, feelings and thoughts about humane treatment are brought out. Our goal as caregivers is to offer comfort and pain relief, regardless of our decisions to forego life sustaining therapy. We worry that having a loved one go through surgery or be placed on a ventilator will be painful and inhumane. These procedures may be painful and inhumane if there is no hope for meaningful life or recovery. They may be very humane if performed with compassion and if they can result in a quality recovery.

Feeding through a tube is another sensitive issue for people to face. Many people after strokes or in the end stage of illness stop eating or can no longer swallow. If a person can't swallow or eat, is it our humane and ethical obligation to offer food through a tube in the nose or stomach? Is doing so extraordinary treatment or basic care? You can keep somebody who is in a coma or vegetative state alive for a long time with tube feeding. Is the *person* still alive, or is only the *body* alive in these situations?

I've worked with many families that don't have trouble deciding not to place a feeding tube in their elderly parent, but when it comes to removing a feeding tube that is already in place, families have difficulty deciding. The result is the same. When the feeding tube is removed, the patient will die from dehydration or malnutrition. The act of not starting something, rather than discontinuing something, seems to make the difference. Some families and doctors decide to place the tube, but provide only water through it, so that the patient won't become dehydrated. There is some controversy about whether death by dehydration is uncomfortable for the patient. Is death by malnutrition any more comfortable? I don't know the answer to these questions. You may have to raise and discuss the questions at some point, however, in your role as a caregiver.

Make an appointment with your parent and her doctor to

discuss these issues in detail, and fill out a durable power of attorney for health care. Be sure to choose someone reliable as the agent to make decisions. An alternate must also be chosen in case the original decision maker is not available. Discuss with the family who the person should be, and be sure that the person chosen is comfortable with the responsibility. Other documents such as advanced directives to physicians and living wills are also available if nobody wants the decision making authority. These documents merely state the patient's preference to withhold or withdraw life-prolonging procedures if the physician has certified that the condition being treated is terminal and death is imminent. With these documents, nobody is given authority to make decisions on behalf of the patient should the patient become incompetent. Whatever advance directive you choose, be sure to give careful consideration to the matter, and from time to time review and update what your parent's wishes are.

Planning in advance of death is important. Knowing how to get through the process of dying can be a tremendous challenge. Death can occur within minutes, hours, days, weeks or months, depending upon individual circumstances. When death is the result of a lengthy terminal illness, the family, caregiver and elderly patient can experience a great burden. Nobody wants a loved one to suffer, and very few people want to be dependent upon others for care. Unfortunately, however, terminal illness often brings dependence, and it sometimes causes discomfort and pain to the elderly person. Chapters 7 and 12 can help you deal with the physical aspects of getting help for an elderly parent who is growing more dependent. You may also investigate Hospice programs. Hospice brings a wide range of services to the home to help families and elderly patients cope with death. Services may include nursing care in the home, health aide care, social work and chaplain services, physician services, medical equipment and supplies, and even bereavement support after death. The goal of hospice care is to offer comfort, dignity, support, and control of pain during the end stages of life. Regulations may vary from state to state, but to qualify for hospice care a physician must state that your elderly parent has no more than six months left to live. Hospice care may be covered under Medicare; you should check with local hospitals or social service agencies to find out if these services are available for your elderly parent.

Many feelings surface when dealing with the death of a parent. Caregivers often emotionally prepare in advance for their loved one's death. The grieving process may begin long before death, when the person for whom we care begins to decline mentally and physically. By the time death approaches, the caregiver may feel that she is not even caring for the same person she once knew. Old age and illness may be cruel, and death in some cases may be a relief to the patient and the caregiver. Don't feel guilty or uncomfortable if at times you wish the person you are caring for would die. These types of thoughts and wishes are not unusual, because none of us likes to see other people suffer—especially people we love and care about.

As children of an aging parent, we often think to ourselves what it would be like to lose our parents. In our minds we may even consider what it would be like if our father outlived our mother or vice versa. If Dad has never cooked for himself or taken care of the house, you will know what to expect if he outlives Mom. You will need to find him help in these areas. If Mom has never paid a bill in her life, never driven a car, or is afraid of being alone, you know what to expect if Mom survives Dad.

Be prepared; speak to your aging parents while they are alive and well about what they would want if they were widowed. You should know as an adult child where all important papers are kept and what, if any, advanced burial arrangements have been made.

You should have wills or living trusts prepared in advance and know where such documents are kept. It may even be wise to have one adult child's signature on necessary bank documents, so that funds can be accessed during incapacity of a parent or after death. One may even go so far as to have an adult child on a property title, so that it can be sold. Estate planning goes far beyond the scope of this book; I recommend consultation with an experienced estate planner for families that have assets to protect or distribute. Ask your lawyer or accountant for recommendations, or look in the phone book for a lawyer or accountant who specializes in estate planning. You may also want to call the elder law attorney association, listed in the Resource Guide at the end of this book, for a referral.

When one elderly parent survives another, adult children who are caregivers must be alert. It is not uncommon for an elderly wife to die very soon after her husband, or for an elderly husband to die very soon after his wife. I have had couples in the nursing home who die within days of each other, even when one of the two was still in relatively good health. Perhaps it is true that a human being can die of a broken heart. After many years of love and marriage, maybe the desire to be together surpasses the natural instinct to survive. Help your surviving parent by increasing your number of visits and encouraging ventilation of feelings. Grief counseling and support groups for widows, widowers, and caregivers may be of some help. Time, love and prayer may be the best medicine for the grieving process.

As a caregiver, you too must adjust after the death of the one for whom you have cared. After your parent dies, you may experience a void in your life, or you may be relieved. If you have been caring for your parent for a long time, you may feel as though you have lost your purpose. Not only will you have empty time to fill, you may experience feelings of loneliness, depression, guilt or anger.

Many caregivers discover, after the death of the one for whom they have cared, that they have isolated themselves during the time of caregiving and no longer have any friends. Recognize and deal with these feelings; reconnect yourself to the world again. Establish your identity and make yourself a priority. Take time to do something for yourself before seeking out a new mission and responsibility. Many caregivers may replace one caregiving situation for another as soon as the opportunity arises, just because caregiving is in their nature. Be careful of over-extending yourself, lest you soon need a caregiver to care for you, due to stress overload.

My staff and I have held the hands of many elderly people and shared their exits from this world. To some death has come swiftly, and to others it was a struggle. With all of our elderly patients and families, it is a privilege to share such a personal experience and to be able to offer love and help. I hope this chapter will someday help you deal with a very trying time in your caregiving mission.

30

ON GROWING OLD

(EPILOGUE)

CAREGIVERS WILL EVENTUALLY GROW OLDER, so learn from your experience of caring for your aging parent; take this advice to heart. Time seems to govern our every action and our total being. Once a second, a minute, an hour, a day, a year, a decade or even a lifetime has passed, it cannot be recovered.

Is growing old a feeling, a concept, or a chronological list of events and years that have passed? Thirty is old to an athlete, yet young for a scholar. Perhaps growing old is only growing old when it presents us with problems or the inability to do what we could when we were younger.

I have found that some grow older gracefully, while others grow older without grace. The road we choose may depend upon our philosophy on life and death; our limited knowledge of the world sets time and aging within a frame which is delineated by birth as a beginning and death as an ending. Maybe the elderly people for whom we care are at an advantage, even when we feel sorry for their ills and misfortunes. If in death there is a new beginning, perhaps the elderly are winners in this journey of life and death.

"Experts" try to tell us how to grow old. Plastic surgeons skillfully remove our wrinkles, bags, droops and fatty deposits. No matter how much we try, however, we cannot halt the forces of nature. To do this would surely bring shame to what was so perfectly created and planned on this earth. How time and aging affects us is molded by our attitudes towards aging.

I exhort you to take care of your body, for it is the only one you will ever have; take care of your soul, for it is the driving force behind your very being. Help others no matter what your age. Your help may leave an everlasting impression on our world and give you reason to rise each morning. Retired or not, cherish work in whatever form your age and ability permit. Work gives meaning to your existence; it connects you to the world.

Let go of past failures and hurts in your life. As the years go by, many of these accumulate. Strive to care for someone or something every day, be it a plant, an animal, or a person. Each day in which your presence is needed in this world is a day which gives you a reason to awaken.

No matter what your age, you should open your mind and curiosity to learn something new, each day. An old dog can be taught new tricks if the reward is worth the effort. No matter how old and set in your ways you may become, occasionally throw caution to the wind and take a chance. The renewed feeling you get from meeting a new challenge may bring back the vigor of youth.

Be sensitive to the balance of giving and receiving. As one grows older, dependence on others may be a principle of nature. Don't be afraid to give, and don't be ashamed to receive. Accept the changes that accompany growing old, and be thankful for every day you have.

Have love and faith, and don't give up until you feel that it's your time. When you do give up, do so with joy. Know that God has a plan for each of us, and that you have fulfilled God's purpose on this earth.

All of us at one time were cared for by someone. Bless the caregivers who care for their aging parents.

In caring for others, don't forget to care for yourself along the way.

RESOURCE GUIDE FOR CAREGIVERS AND THEIR ELDERLY LOVED ONES

As discussed throughout this book, access to good information is essential to the caregiver's success. There are many public and private organizations and associations available to assist you in your *caregiver's mission*. Sometimes getting the information and support you need will require several phone calls, and multiple inquiries to many agencies. My advice to caregivers: ***Don't give up until you find answers to your questions.***

Here are some tips to help you get the information you need.

☞ Write down your questions before you make the call.

☞ Ask and write down the name and number of the person you speak with, for future reference, and document what was said so that you can properly use the information.

☞ Ask them to mail you written materials about their organization and how it helps caregivers and the elderly for whom they provide care.

☞ Ask them the mission and purpose of their organization.

☞ Ask if there are local chapters available in your community that may be of help to you.

☞ Ask if there is a charge for their services.

☞ Ask if their organization has public funds available to provide assistance to you.

☞ If the person you call does not have an answer to your questions, ask if he/she knows someone within the organization or in a different organization who can help.

☞ You may not always get through on your first call, but don't give up. You may want to avoid calling public agencies on Monday mornings, Friday afternoons, around the lunch hours and before and after holidays. If you call at these times, it may be difficult to get through.

All the information and support in the world is of no value if the caregiver does not accept the help. Most of the organizations listed are non-profit agencies which were created and are operated in order to meet a special need. *Please let them help if they can.*

The following listings of organizations are for informational purposes only. Listing of any specific organization does not imply approval or endorsement by the author or publisher of *The Caregiver's Mission.*

STATE AGENCIES ON AGING

At the Federal level of government, the Department of Health and Human Services' Administration on Aging oversees the coordination of aging services throughout the country. The State Agencies on Aging oversee the coordination of aging services within each state. At the local or community level, there are approximately 670 Area Agencies on Aging, which may be of assistance to caregivers and their elderly loved ones. You can locate your local Area Agency on Aging by finding the phone number in your phone book or by calling the appropriate State Agency on Aging we have listed for you.

Services Which Area Agencies on Aging
May Coordinate In Your Community

☞ referrals to services and providers you may need

☞ assistance in assessing the needs of your elderly loved one

☞ assistance in planning and monitoring care for your loved one

☞ information and assistance with transportation needs

☞ information on adult day care in your area

☞ information on home delivered meals in your area

☞ information on senior centers and their services in your area

☞ information on legal services available in your area

☞ information on home care services that may be available to you in your area

☞ information on telephone reassurance programs or friendly visit programs

☞ information on emergency alert response systems in your area that connect your elderly loved one to help by pressing a button that is linked to a local hospital or monitoring station

☞ information on respite care services in your community

☞ information on nursing homes, and board and care facilities in your area

☞ information on ombudsman services in your community if your loved one is in a long-term care facility and you have a complaint and concern that you need assistance with

☞ information on agencies that coordinate conservatorships, adult protective services and various mental health and social issues relevant to care of the elderly

☞ information on financial and public assistance programs that may be available to you, such as Medicaid

State Agencies on Aging

Alabama
Commission on Aging
770 Washington Avenue
Montgomery AL 36130
Toll Free (within state)
1-800-243-5463
(205) 242-5743

Alaska
Older Alaskans Commission
P.O. Box C, MS 0209
Juneau AK 99811
(907) 465-3250

American Samoa
Territorial Admin. on Aging
Govt. of American Samoa
Pago Pago AS 96799
(684) 633-1251

Arizona
Dept. of Economic Security
Aging and Adult Administration
1400 W. Washington Stret
Phoenix AZ 85007
(602) 542-4446

Arkansas
Div. of Aging and Adult Services
Donaghey Plaza South
Suite 1417
7th and Main Streets
P.O. Box 1417/Slot 1412
Little Rock AR 72203-1437
(501) 682-2441

California
Department of Aging
1600 K Street
Sacramento CA 95814
(916) 322-3887

Colorado
Aging and Adult Services
Department of Social Services
1575 Sherman Street
10th Floor
Denver CO 80203-1714
(303) 866-3851

Commonwealth of the
    Northern Mariana Islands
Dept. of Community and
    Cultural Affairs
Civic Center
Commonwealth of the
    Northern Mariana Islands
Saipan CM 96950
(607) 234-6011

Connecticut
Dept. on Aging
175 Main Street
Hartford CT 06106
Toll Free (within state)
1-800-443-9946
(203) 566-7772

Delaware
Division of Aging
Dept. of Health and Social Services
1901 N. DuPont Highway
New Castle DE 19720
(302) 421-6791

District of Columbia
Office on Aging
1424 K Street, N.W., 2nd Floor
Washington DC 20005
(202) 724-5626
(202) 724-5622

Federated States of Micronesia
State Agency on Aging
Office of Health Services
Federated States of Micronesia
Ponape E.C.I. 96941

Florida
Office of Aging and Adult Services
1317 Winewood Boulevard
Tallahassee FL 32301
(904) 488-8922

Georgia
Office of Aging
Department of Human Resources
878 Peachtree Street, N.E.
Room 632
Atlanta GA 30309
(404) 894-5333

Guam
Division of Senior Citizens
Department of Public Health and
  Social Services
P.O. Box 2816
Agana GU 96910
(671) 734-4361

Hawaii
Executive Office on Aging
335 Merchant Street
Room 241
Honolulu HI 96813
(808) 586-0100

Idaho
Office on Aging
Statehouse, Room 108
Boise ID 83720
(208) 334-3833

Illinois
Department on Aging
421 E. Capitol Avenue
Springfield IL 62701
(217) 785-2870

Indiana
Department of Human Services
251 North Illinois Street
P.O. Box 7083
Indianapolis IN 46207-7083
(317) 232-7020

Iowa
Department of Elder Affairs
Jewett Building, Suite 236
914 Grand Avenue
Des Moines IA 50319
(515) 281-5187

Kansas
Department on Aging
122-S Docking State Office Building
915 S.W. Harrison
Topeka KS 66612-1500
(913) 296-4986

Kentucky
Division for Aging Services
Department for Social Services
275 E. Main Street
Frankfort KY 40621
(502) 564-6930

Louisiana
Governor's Office of Elderly Affairs
P.O. Box 80374
Baton Rouge LA 70898-0374
(504) 925-1700

Maine
Bureau of Elder & Adult Services
State House, Station 11
Augusta ME 04333
(207) 624-5335

Maryland
State Agency on Aging
301 W. Preston Street, Room 1004
Baltimore MD 21201
(301) 225-1102

Masschusetts
Executive Office of Elder Affairs
38 Chauncy Street
Boston MA 02111
Toll Free (within state)
1-800-882-2003
(617) 727-7750

Michigan
Office of Services to the Aging
P.O. Box 30026
Lansing MI 48909
(517) 373-8230

Minnesota
Minnesota Board on Aging
Human Services Building
4th Floor
444 Lafayette Road
St. Paul MN 55155-3843
(612) 296-2770

Mississippi
Council on Aging
421 W. Pascagoula Street
Jackson MS 39203-3524
Toll Free (within state)
1-800-222-7622
(601) 949-2070

Missouri
Division of Aging
Department of Social Services
P.O. Box 1337 -
   615 Howerton Court
Jefferson MO 65102-1337
(314) 751-3082

Montana
The Governor's
   Office on Aging
State Capital Building, Room 219
Helena MT 59620
Toll Free (within state)
1-800-332-2272
(406) 444-3111

Nebraska
Department on Aging
State Office Building
301 Centennial Mall South
Lincoln NE 68509
(402) 471-2306

Nevada
Department of Human Resources
Division for Aging Services
340 N. 11th Street, Suite 114
Las Vegas NV 89101
(702) 687-4210

New Hampshire
Department of Health
   and Human Services
Division of Elderly
   and Adult Services
6 Hazan Drive
Concord NH 03301
(603) 271-4680

New Jersey
Department of Community Affairs
Division on Aging
S. Broad and Front Sts., CN 807
Trenton NJ 08625-0807
Toll Free (within state)
1-800-792-8820
(609) 292-0920

New Mexico
Agency on Aging
La Villa Rivera Bldg., 4th Floor
224 E. Palace Avenue
Santa Fe NM 87501
Toll Free (within state)
1-800-432-2080
(505) 827-7640

New York
State Office for the Aging
2 Empire State Plaza
Albany NY 12223-0001
Toll Free (within state)
1-800-342-9871
(518) 474-5731

North Carolina
Department of Human Resources
Division of Aging
693 Palmer Drive
Raleigh NC 27626-0531
(919) 733-3983

North Dakota
Department of Human Services
Aging Services Division
State Capitol Building
Bismarck ND 58505
(701) 224-2577

Ohio
Department of Aging
50 W. Broad Street
8th Floor
Columbus OH 43266-0501
(614) 466-1221

Oklahoma
Department of Human Services
Aging Services Division
P.O. Box 25352
Oklahoma City OK 73125
(405) 521-2327

Oregon
Department of Human Resources
Senior Services Division
313 Public Service Building
Salem OR 97310
Toll Free (within state)
1-800-232-3020
(503) 378-4728

Palau
State Agency on Aging
Department of Social Services
Republic of Palau
Koror, Palau 96940

Pennsylvania
Department of Aging
231 State Street
Barto Building
Harrisburg PA 17101
(717) 783-1550

Puerto Rico
Governors Office of Elderly Affairs
Gericulture Commission
Box 11398
Santurce PR 00910
(809) 722-2429 or 722-0225

Republic of the Marshall Islands
State Agency on Aging
Department of Social Services
Republic of the Marshall Islands
Marjuro, Marshall Islands 96960

Rhode Island
Department of Elderly Affairs
160 Pine Street
Providence RI 02903
(401) 277-2858

South Carolina
Commission on Aging
400 Arbor Lake Drive
Suite B-500
Columbia SC 29223
(803) 735-0210

South Dakota
Agency on Aging
Adult Services and Aging
Richard F. Kneip Building
700 Governors Drive
Pierre SD 57501-2291
(605) 773-3656

Tennessee
Commission on Aging
706 Church Street
Suite 201
Nashville TN 37219-5573
(615) 741-2056

Texas
Department on Aging
P.O. Box 12786
Capitol Station
Austin TX 78741-3702
(512) 444-2727

Utah
Division of Aging
  and Adult Services
120 North 200 West
P.O. Box 45500
Salt Lake City UT 84145-0500
(801) 538-3910

Vermont
Office on Aging
Waterbury Complex
103 S. Main Street
Waterbury VT 05676
(802) 241-2400

Virginia
Department for the Aging
700 Centre, 10th Floor
700 E. Franklin Street
Richmond VA 23219-2327
Toll Free (within state)
1-800-552-4464
(804) 225-2271

Virgin Islands
Department of Human Services
19 Estate Diamond Frederick Sted
St. Croix VI 00840
(809) 772-4850

Washington
Aging & Adult Services
   Administration
Department of Social
   and Health Services
Mail Stop OB-44-A
Olympia WA 98504
(206) 586-3768

West Virginia
Commission on Aging
State Capitol Complex
Holly Grove
Charleston WV 25305
Toll Free (within state)
1-800-642-3671
(304) 348-3317

Wisconsin
Bureau on Aging
Department of Health
   and Social Services
P.O. Box 7851
Madison WI 53707
Toll Free (within state)
1-800-242-1060
(608) 266-2536

Wyoming
Commission on Aging
Hathaway Building
First Floor
Cheyenne WY 82002
Toll Free (within state)
1-800-442-2766
(307) 777-7986

Alzheimer's Disease

Alzheimer's Association National Headquarters
919 North Michigan Avenue, Suite 1000
Chicago, Illinois 60611-1676
(312) 335-8700   1-800-272-3900
Provides information and referrals to services in the community. Over 200 nationwide chapters with nearly 1,600 support groups throughout the country.

Alzheimer's Disease Education & Referral Center
P.O. Box 8250
Silver Spring MD 20907-8250
1-800-438-4380, (301) 495-3311
Provides information to assist those caring for Alzheimer's victims as well as referrals to needed resources.

Arthritis

Arthritis Foundation
1314 Spring Street, N.W.
Atlanta GA 30309
1-800-283-7800
Provides educational materials and referrals to support services for those suffering from arthritis.

Caregiver Support

Children of Aging Parents (CAP)
2761 Trenton Road
Levittown PA 19056
(215) 945-6900
Provides information and support to caregivers of aging parents as well as information on how to find local support groups in your area.

National Federation of Interfaith Volunteer Caregivers
105 Marry's Avenue
P.O. Box 10139
Kingston NY 12401
(914) 331-1358
Provides education, support services to the elderly and their caregivers.

National Association of Private Geriatric Care Managers
   655 N. Alvernon Way, Suite 108
   Tucson AZ 85711
   (602) 881-8008

   A Geriatric Care Manager is a professional who assists caregivers and their elderly loved ones to assess needs and connect those needs to appropriate support services. Care managers are often available to manage care for an elderly loved one, especially if the family lives far away from the older adult needing care. If someone tells you he/she is a geriatric care manager, be sure that the person has the proper training and experience in eldercare services. The National Association of Private Geriatric Care Managers may refer you to an appropriately trained geriatric care manager in your community.

Diabetes

American Diabetes Association
   1660 Duke Street
   Alexandria VA 22314
   1-800-232-3472

   Provides educational materials on diabetes and information on support groups for diabetics.

National Diabetes Information Clearing House
   Box NDIC
   Bethesda MD 20892
   (301) 468-2162

   Provides information on diabetes.

Emergency Response

Lifeline Systems Inc.
   1 Arsenal Market Place
   Watertown MA 02172
   1-800-543-3546

   Provides personal emergency alert response systems whereby your elderly loved one can press a button on a bracelet or necklace that activates an alarm monitored by a local hospital monitoring station. When alarm is received, help is called. These types of systems are designed to give you and your elderly loved one peace of mind should a fall or medical emergency occur when no one is around to help. Lifeline Systems may have local monitoring services in your community.

Medic Alert Foundation
P.O. Box 1009
Turlock CA 95381
(209) 668-3333
Provides medic alert bracelets that an elderly patient wears around the wrist in case of an emergency. The medic alert bracelet gives the phone number of the foundation which keeps a record of your elderly loved one's medical problems, history, medications, and identifying information. *If your elderly loved one suffers from memory loss, you should get him/her a medic alert bracelet. If he/she wanders away and gets lost or injured, appropriate information will be available to provide help if a medic alert bracelet is worn.*

Hearing Difficulties

National Association of the Deaf
814 Thayer Avenue
Silver Spring MD 20901
(301) 587-1899
Provides education, information and support for those with hearing impairments.

Self Help for the Hard of Hearing
4848 Battery Lane, Suite 100
Bethesda MD 20814
(301) 657-2248
Provides information and support for the hard of hearing.

National Hearing Aid Society
20361 Middlebelt Street
Livonia MI 48152
(313) 478-2610

Heart Disease and Strokes

American Heart Association
7320 Greenville Avenue
Dallas TX 75231
(214) 373-6300
Provides education and information on heart problems and stroke.

Courage Stroke Network
   3915 Golden Valley Road
   Golden Valley MN 55422
   1-800-553-6321, (612) 558-0811
   Provides information and support services to stroke victims
   and their caregivers.

National Stroke Association
   300 E. Hampden Avenue, Suite 240
   Englewood CO 80110
   (303) 762-992
   Provides education, information and support services for
   stroke victims and their caregivers.

Hospice Care & Bereavement Issues

Foundation for Hospice & Homecare
   519 C Street, N.W.
   Washington DC 20002
   (202) 547-6586

National Hospice Organization
   1901 North Moore Street, Suite 901
   Arlington VA 22209
   (703) 243-5900

Hospice Education Institute
   5 Essex Square, Suite 3B
   Essex CT 06426
   1-800-331-1620, (203) 767-1620
   Provides referrals to hospice services in your area.

They Help Each Other Spiritually
   717 Liberty Avenue
   1301 Clark Building
   Pittsburgh PA 15222
   (412) 471-7779
   Provides information and support after the loss of a loved one.

Incontinence

Simon Foundation
   P.O. Box 835
   Wilmette IL 60091
   1-800-237-4666
   Provides information and support for those suffering with
   incontinence.

Legal Services

The National Association of Elder Law Attorneys
655 N. Alvernon Way, #108
Tucson AZ 85711
(602) 881-4005
If Medicaid or estate planning is needed, it is important for caregivers to seek the counsel of an attorney who *specializes* in elder law. Members of this organization have a special interest in elder law. You may call them to get more information about how to choose an elder law attorney and they may refer you to one of their members.

Parkinson's Disease

American Parkinson's Disease Association
60 Bay Street, Suite 401
Staten Island NY 10301
1-800-223-2371 outside of NY, (718) 981-8001
Provides information, support and referrals on Parkinson's Disease.

National Parkinson's Foundation
1501 NW 9th Avenue
Miami FL 33136-1494
1-800-327-4545, (305) 547-6666

Parkinson's Disease Foundation
650 W 168th Street
New York NY 10032
1-800-456-6676, (212) 923-4700

Parkinson's Educational Program U.S.A.
3900 Birch, Suite 105
Newport Beach CA 92660
1-800-344-7872, (714) 640-0218

Parkinson's Support Groups of America
11376 Cherry Hill Road, Suite 204
Beltsville MD 20705
(301) 937-1545

United Parkinson Foundation
360 W. Superior Street
Chicago IL 60610
(312) 664-2344

Resources and Services for the Visually Impaired

American Foundation for the Blind
15 W 16th Street
New York NY 10011
1-800-232-5463, (212) 620-2000
Information and support services for the blind.

National Association for the Visually Handicapped
22 W 21st Street
New York NY 10010
(212) 889-2141
Information and support services for the blind.

Vision Foundation, Inc.
818 Mt. Auburn Street
Watertown MA 02172
1-800-852-3029 (MA toll free number), (617)
926-4232
Provides catalog of resources to assist those with low vision.

Visions
817 Broadway, 11th Floor
New York NY 10003
(212) 477-3800
Offers information, support services and professional support
to the blind.

Associated Services for the Blind
919 Walnut Street
Philadelphia PA 19107
(215) 627-0600
Provides subscriptions to popular magazines such as Family
Circle, as well as books on tapes and mail order supplies for
the blind.

Books on Tape
P.O. Box 7900
Newport Beach CA 92658-7900
1-800-626-3333
Provides books on tape for the visually impaired.

Braille Circulating Library
2700 Stuart Avenue
Richmond VA 23220
(804) 359-3743
Provides talking books, large print books and other material
for the blind.

Choice Magazine Listening
  85 Channel Drive
  Port Washington NY 11050
  (516) 883-8280
  Offers articles from popular magazines on tape cassettes.

John Milton Society for the Blind
  475 Riverside Drive, Room 455
  New York NY 10115
  (212) 870-3335
  Provides Christian literature in large type.

Library of Congress National Library Service for the Blind
  1291 Taylor Street, N.W.
  Washington DC 20542
  1-800-424-8567, (202) 707-5100
  Provides free talking book services to the visually impaired.

Jewish Braille Institute of America
  110 E 30th Street
  New York NY 10016
  (212) 889-2525
  Provides talking books and publishes information for the blind.

Xavier Society for the Blind
  154 E 23rd Street
  New York NY 10010
  (212) 473-7800
  Produces the Catholic Review in large print and on tape.

American Bible Society
  1865 Broadway
  New York NY 10023
  (212) 408-1200
  Publishes the scriptures in large print and recorded forms.

American Printing House for the Blind
  1839 Frankfort Avenue
  P.O. Box 6085
  Louisville KY 40206-0085
  (502) 895-2405
  Provides free subscriptions to *Newsweek, Reader's Digest,* and other information on tape.

Bible Alliance, Inc.
P.O. Box 621
Bradenton FL 34206
(813) 748-3031
Provides the scriptures recorded in 33 languages for free on casette tapes to the visually impaired.

Reader's Digest/Large Type Edition
P.O. Box 241
Mount Morris IL 60154
(815) 734-6963
Provides subscription to large print *Reader's Digest.*

Ulverscroft Large Print Books
279 Boston Street
Guilford CT 06437
(203) 453-2080
Sells large print books directly to the public.

Independent Living Aids
27 E. Mall
Plainview NY 11803
(516) 752-8080
Produces a catalog of devices to help the visually impaired cope with daily living.

The Lighthouse Low Vision Products
3602 Northern Blvd.
Long Island City NY 11101
1-800-453-4923
Provides devices and equipment to aid the blind.

If *The Caregiver's Mission* provided you the information
and support you needed to succeed as a caregiver,
why not get a copy for a family member or friend
who has also been touched by the
responsibilities of caring for
an elderly loved one?

To order additional copies of
The Caregiver's Mission by Steven Ross,
please send your check or money order for
$15.95 postpaid for each copy ordered to:

DISTINCTIVE PUBLISHING CORP.
P.O. Box 17868
Plantation FL 33318-7868
(305) 975-2413

Quantity discounts are also available
from the publisher.

If you would like to send your personal comments
to the author, you may do so by
writing to the above address.
We would appreciate hearing from you.